IS IT SUCCESS
OR IS IT ADDICTION?

IS IT SUCCESS? OR IS IT ADDICTION?

THOMAS PIKE & WILLIAM PROCTOR

THOMAS NELSON PUBLISHERS
Nashville

Published in Nashville, Tennessee, by Thomas Nelson, Inc., and distributed in Canada by Lawson Falle, Ltd., Cambridge, Ontario.

Printed in the United States of America.

Scripture quotations are from THE NEW KING JAMES VERSION of the Bible. Copyright © 1979, 1980, 1982, Thomas Nelson, Inc., Publishers.

ISBN 0-8407-7605-5

1 2 3 4 5 6 — 92 91 90 89 88

CONTENTS

PREFACE

It's difficult to write a book on the meaning of success without drawing upon your own experiences and the experiences of those you know well. As a result I've delved into my own attitudes, beliefs and struggles, and those of other men and women who have dealt with the issues and problems that accompany an orientation toward achievement.

When I've referred to other people, I've taken pains in every case to disguise their identities by changing their sex, backgrounds, or other key features. In fact, I have gone over every passage several times to be certain that the real people would be completely masked, and some of the most sensitive examples have been presented as composite experiences. I believe adamantly that the counseling relationship should remain confidential, and I've made every effort to uphold this conviction.

As you read the following pages, I trust that the lessons and lives of those I've described will help you in some way to attain significant satisfaction—and true success—in your own upward movement.

Thomas Pike

IS IT SUCCESS
OR IS IT ADDICTION?

THE RISE OF A RELIGION OF SUCCESS

On the surface Sam and Vicki seemed the perfect couple, the epitome of the American ideal of success and happiness. A highly accomplished forty-year-old attorney, Sam had risen to the position of partner in a prestigious big-city law firm, and he was now pulling in an annual compensation of nearly $300,000. Vicki, a thirty-eight-year-old Harvard MBA, had recently been made vice president of a Fortune 500 company, and with her salary and investments, she brought the family income up to more than $500,000 a year.

Their considerable financial means enabled them to own three homes: a huge condominium in the city, a country estate, and a villa in the Bahamas. As for cars they usually settled for his-and-her Mercedes, though occasionally Vicki would trade down to a Jaguar or BMW. Also, Sam and Vicki *looked* good—slim from regular jogging, swimming, and tennis; tanned from frequent weekend jaunts to island resorts; and dressed to the teeth in expensive, high-fashion clothing.

To top off the family image, the couple's two children, Mark and Heather, already seemed on a fast track to success, even though they were only eight and six years old, respectively. Both attended the best private schools, took music lessons from the most desirable teachers, engaged in all sorts of athletic activities under the tutelage of private coaches and, like their parents, kept busy in a swirl of appointments from dawn to dusk.

Sam, Vicki, Mark, and Heather were the ideal family, the personification of the Great American Success Story—or so it seemed on the surface. But what about *underneath* the surface? What was going on below that seemingly perfect facade of achievement, wealth, and physical beauty?

When they decided to seek counseling, I quickly became aware that the veneer of success in their lives was already beginning to crack. Although Sam had achieved a great deal in his career, he was now wondering, *Where do I go from here?*

Also, having just passed the forty-year-old mark, he had begun to sense his own mortality. Despite his relatively good physical condition, he was beginning to lose his hair and was having some trouble keeping his waist as slim as it once had been. Apparently in response to these worries about advancing age, he had become deeply involved in an extramarital affair with a twenty-five-year-old, and he was even contemplating divorce.

Vicki, though unaware of Sam's escapades, knew he was feeling out of sorts with his life. And for that matter, she had her own dissatisfactions. Although she received plenty of positive reinforcement about her "marvelous and enviable" career and family position, as one friend put it, she really wasn't so sure that her situation was all it was cracked up to be.

"You really have it all," another friend exclaimed practically every time she and Vicki got together. Vicki had heard such trendy platitudes too often to accept them at face value. Instead she had begun to ask herself, *What exactly* do *I have?*

And the answer that kept coming up was this: *I have a lot of things. Also, I have a lot of short-lived accolades and ephemeral words of admiration. But what else do I have? What do I possess that is really lasting and meaningful?*

Vicki was the first to perceive the treacherous path that she and her husband were treading. She began to feel guilty that in their single-minded striving for success, they had neglected their own relationship and their relationship with their children.

Both spouses typically spent a minimum of twelve hours a day in work and commuting time, and often they put in longer hours. Then, there were the frequent out-of-town trips. As a result of this heavy work schedule, they spent very little time with each other. When they were together, they usually were so exhausted or preoccupied that they didn't communicate, other than on a very superficial level.

Because they had organized their lives so as to give their work a top priority, they found they had no choice but to leave their children in the care of a round of baby sitters and governesses, many of whom were poorly educated. More often than not, when one child-care person left their employ, they didn't even take the time or exert the energy to do a good job of interviewing the next candidate. After a cursory interview, they usually just hired whoever seemed adequate for the job.

I wish I could say that the problems faced by this family turned out just fine. I wish I could tell you that they saw that their priorities were out of whack and they took decisive steps to correct the situation—and lived happily ever after. But unfortunately, that's not what happened.

Sam became totally infatuated with the twenty-five-year-old and eventually asked for a divorce, which he got after a messy legal battle. His second marriage lasted about five years and also ended in divorce for many of the same reasons that had caused the first to crumble. Vicki tried to heal and forget her emotional wounds by plunging ever deeper into her career. She succeeded only in burying her head in the sand and neglecting other problems, especially those involving her children. The youngsters did poorly at school and developed a variety of psychological ills and insecurities as a result of the difficulties at home.

As we look at the situation faced by Sam, Vicki, and their children, we can probably see bits and pieces of problems we have faced in our careers and home lives. But what we're dealing with here cuts far deeper into our culture and our personal lives than most of us realize. If we go to the very essence of what was wrong with this particular family, we see an upwardly mobile man and woman who had unknowingly become trapped in a way of thinking and behaving that I call the *American Success Cult*.

What exactly is this American Success Cult? We'll be delving into a more complete examination of the phenomenon later, but for now a brief description will suffice.

A number of success gurus in our culture, including popular writers, positive thinkers, and top achievers in a variety of fields, tell us through word and example that the *most important thing in life is to acquire the outward trappings of achievement:* to move up a career ladder, accumulate a lot of wealth, "realize your greatest potential," or whatever. Those who promote this viewpoint are the leaders of the Cult.

These *Cult leaders are unequivocal in claiming that they have a complete corner on the truth,* and they stand ready to deride anyone who offers a radically different road to happiness and satisfaction. If you've ever tried to go against the Success Cult's mind-set, you know the typical responses:

"Every successful person has to expect to make personal sacrifices."

"Of course it's important for everyone to try to reach the top!"

"Winning is not something—it's everything!"

"If you expect to succeed, your career must come first!"

"A mature spouse should always understand the demands of a mate's job."

"Children who are benignly neglected have a way of turning out all right."

Members of the Cult also receive intense indoctrination and constant supervision. How does this happen? Spend a day or so observing what goes on in a typical high-pressured corporation, law firm, university, or other workplace, and you'll see what I mean. The upwardly mobile Cult members spend long hours on the job, and their minds and emotions are constantly bombarded with the cultic ethic: Achieve! Succeed! Always be at your peak performance! Strive for excellence! Beat the competition!

There's little time or opportunity to step back from the heavy focus on fast-track achievement and ask, What's happening to me and my attitudes? Are my values being shaped in a healthy, productive way, in a way I really want them to be shaped?

Finally, the *values of the Cult tend to encroach upon and compromise the orthodox doctrines* and work of traditional religion, especially Christianity and Judaism.

For example, Jesus said, "You cannot serve God and mammon,"[1] or material wealth. But gurus of the American Success Cult would take a different slant. They might argue, "You *can* believe in God and worship the almighty dollar simultaneously! Try it and see!"

Or they might just say boldly, "Hey, forget that radical religious nonsense! God is for pie-in-the-sky by-and-by. Supersuccess, high-profile status, and megabuck investments are for *now!*"

But there's an even more insidious development afoot. The Success Cult has also crept into much of organized religion without many priests, pastors, or parishioners being aware of what's happening. Listen, for example, to various TV preachers, religious talk-show hosts, popular Christian writers—and even many local pastors—and you'll encounter more of a gospel of riches and prosperity than *the* gospel of salvation, sacrifice, servanthood, and the Cross.

How often we see rows of expensive cars parked in front of our opulent churches or religious facilities. How often we become swelled with pride as we survey packed pews filled with well-dressed church members—and maybe a celebrity or two. And how often we hear preachers and congregation members alike saying:

"God wants you to be blessed with health and wealth!"

"I *deserve* to be well-paid!"

"God never intended His faithful to go wanting."

"If you'll just believe, you'll receive your heart's desire."

"If you're facing hard times financially, give to my ministry, and God will respond with material rewards."

Yet how infrequently we hear these words of the real gospel:

"Whoever desires to become great among you, let him be your servant."[2]

"He who finds his life will lose it, and he who loses his life for My sake will find it."[3]

"It is easier for a camel to go through the eye of a needle than for a rich man to enter the kingdom of God."[4]

"But those who desire to be rich fall into temptation."[5]

"For the love of money is a root of all kinds of evil."[6]

"I know how to be abased . . . I have learned the secret of facing hunger . . . and want."[7]

"Foxes have holes and birds of the air have nests, but the Son of Man has nowhere to lay his head."[8]

The American Success Cult has usurped these fundamental teachings of Jesus and the apostles and has substituted its own set of beliefs and doctrines.

I tack the word *American* onto *Success Cult,* by the way, only because the United States of America is the main place where capitalism, materialism, and the Protestant work ethic have gone completely haywire. This is not to say that the Success Cult doesn't exist in other advanced lands and cultures, because it most assuredly does. But the contemporary American version sets the standard for superachieving, ambition-obsessed insanity.

Let's look a little more closely at this phenomenon. Let's see how it evolved and how it has taken on the trappings of a modern-day religious faith. Then you'll be in a better position to understand how the Cult may in some ways have taken hold of *your* life.

CHAPTER TWO

THE ROOTS OF THE "FAITH"

One of the most common complaints I hear among ambitious, upscale men and women these days is that there's something wrong with their jobs or careers. Words like these echo through my study, day after day:

"I can't seem to find the right career."

"I don't know what to do with my life."

"I know what I want to do, but why aren't there any openings?"

"How do I find out what God wants me to do with my life?"

"I'm in my chosen field, but it looks like I won't make it to the top—and that's extremely frustrating."

"I've achieved all I hoped to achieve, but is this all there is to life? What's next?"

Most people these days have been fooled into thinking that the most important thing in their lives is, or should be, their jobs. They assume that somehow they can find ultimate meaning in their careers. Also, those who have a religious faith often believe—quite erroneously—that the main thing they should expect from God in life is the perfect job. When He fails to give it to them (or they fail to find it), they get very anxious and unhappy.

The main reason we have these feelings and frustrations is that we have become, to one extent or another, enslaved by the beliefs and assumptions of the American Success Cult. To understand better why we have been ensnared by this destructive mind-set and to learn how to escape, we will trace the roots of the problem back to their source.

The modern expression of the Cult didn't just pop up overnight full-blown and without precedent. Historically, the American Success Cult is the product of powerful forces as old as humankind.

The book of Genesis contains the classic Judeo-Christian statement of how the human relationship to work got started. After the creation, God placed man in the Garden of Eden and told him to keep it and till it. But after the Fall, the pleasure and joy of this work apparently disappeared. Part of man's punishment was to labor over the ground "in toil" and "in the sweat of [his] face."[1]

Still, many of those who were favored by God after the Fall—including the patriarchs Abraham, Isaac, Jacob, and Joseph, the kings David and Solomon, and others—eventually became prosperous and attained great prestige and social status. To be sure they all faced anxieties, difficulties, and hard times, but God blessed them with material possessions and community respect.

Unfortunately, however, the temporal success of these Old Testament figures, as well as some later leaders of the Christian era, has caused many people to lose perspective on wealth, status, and success. It's been too easy to take these great human examples, couple them with isolated scriptural passages in Proverbs and elsewhere, and formulate a gospel of riches and success.

What exactly do the Bible and historic Christianity say about the believer and the meaning of success?

First of all, the lives of great and godly leaders in the Old Testament certainly do confirm that being successful may be all right with God. In fact, He may provide a believer with material blessings. Proverbs tells us, "A faithful man will abound with blessings," and "In all labor there is profit, / But idle chatter leads only to poverty."[2] Furthermore, Proverbs says a talented worker may expect status and respect: "Do you see a man who excels in his work? / He will stand before kings; / He will not stand before unknown men."[3]

Faithfulness to God, hard work, and good training—these are qualities God may bless with temporal success. But do we have a right to expect success if we just meet these criteria?

A closer look at the Bible gives us a more complex picture. Even those patriarchs, kings, and other great Old Testament figures often encountered hardships and tragedies. Jacob had to flee his home to escape the wrath of an angry brother. Joseph was sold into slavery. And David hid out in caves and was forced to fight his sons for power.

In the New Testament the ancient Hebrew emphasis on the importance of hard work continues. The apostle Paul urged the church members in Thessalonica to aspire to live quietly and work with their hands so that they could earn the respect of outsiders and be independent.[4] Not only that, he warned them to work hard and avoid those who remained idle. "If anyone will not work, neither shall he eat,"[5] Paul said.

As both Jesus and Paul indicate, God will respond bountifully to those who give cheerfully and freely.[6] At the same time, however—as we've already seen in our reference to the modern-day gospel of wealth—there are many warnings about accumulating riches or focusing upon them. In fact, most passages of the New Testament that deal with wealth urge and extol the act of giving it away rather than piling it up!

Still, the biblical approach to success, including the acquisition of wealth, fame, and power, is not simple. So it's understandable that in postbiblical times, individuals have been faced with considerable distortion and confusion about God's will for earthly success.

At times believers have heard a call to simplicity and to renunciation of worldly goods. St. Francis of Assisi, who gave up great wealth and position to follow Jesus, has been a model for many, both past and present. Even Thomas Aquinas, that urbane and (by most worldly standards) successful medieval theologian and philosopher, placed his success lower than many people in his position might.

One day, for example, he went to worship in a humble church with a group of very lowly Christians. As they all stood around the table, waiting to take Holy Communion, he looked up and noticed that the volumes of his great *Summa Theologica* were on a nearby bookshelf. Yet as he compared his life's work as a career theologian to his relationship with those individual Christians, he gestured toward the books and said, "It's all straw—all straw."

One of the major reasons this perspective on

achievement and wealth has been lost is that we have distorted the real meaning of the concept of the "calling." When you hear the word *calling*, chances are that it's synonymous in your mind with *job* or *career*. That's what has happened to the concept of calling in the last few centuries, and this development is one of the most insidious ingredients in the rise of the Success Cult.

Actually, the idea of a call or calling has solid roots in the New Testament, where the term usually refers to the call of a person to faith in Christ. Paul wrote to the Romans that God has called those whom He has chosen to be glorified with His Son.[7] And Paul told Timothy that God "called us with a holy calling" to work for Him as ministers of the gospel.[8] Furthermore, Paul saw the calling characterized by the Christian virtues of humility, patience, and unity in God's Spirit.

Nothing about money here! Nor anything about power, fame, or worldly success. Indeed, anyone would be hard put to equate the biblical idea of calling with a secular career.

But in the years since the Bible was written, something strange has happened. Gradually, among both religious thinkers and secular pundits, calling has been equated with career, including career success and satisfaction. How did this happen?

Ambition and materialism have always been parts of human nature, whether before or after Christ. A monarch of the Middle Ages, King Pippin, once asked the Christian monk Alcuin, "Of what have men never enough?"

Alcuin's reply: "Of gain."

Later, during the time of Martin Luther and John Calvin, the debate heated up over whether and how God called a person to a particular money-making profession or enterprise. Luther came to regard the calling as "the labor of the secular, everyday, God-appointed task," according to Professor Kemper Fullerton, a theologian who wrote for *The Harvard Theological Review* in 1928. An expert on Max Weber, the author of the classic *Protestant Ethic and the Spirit of Capitalism*, Fullerton noted that the Calvinists, and especially the Puritans, expanded further upon the idea of the calling. Specifically, they saw the calling as:

- a life of strict discipline;
- a life focusing on work in the secular world;
- a life with the sole intention of glorifying God; and
- a life in which productive secular work and service would act as proof that the individual had truly been saved and could expect heaven as the ultimate reward.

Clearly, then, even though this Puritan idea of the calling had become closely connected with secular work and careers, it retained a spiritual dimension. God was definitely involved in how daily work, including the accumulation of wealth and the achievement of success, was to be regarded and pursued. Those engaged in a calling were expected to use their time well, avoid sloth, be good stewards of God's largesse and, in general, observe near-ascetic standards of spending their wealth upon themselves. Accumulation of capital was okay, but conspicuous personal consumption was not.

There were dangers in these developments. It's only human nature to want to spend money when you make it. After all, it's *yours,* isn't it—even if God had something to do with providing it through His calling?

John Wesley, the great eighteenth-century evangelist and founder of Methodism, saw the danger. "I fear whenever riches have increased, the essence of religion has decreased in the same proportion," he said in one of his sermons.

As if on cue, the great secularist money manager Benjamin Franklin appeared at about the same time to promote the idea of the calling as an end in itself. Franklin freely quoted the Bible, especially Proverbs. But his main purpose was to show that hard work, shrewd judgment, and highly honed skills were essential because people have a responsibility to make as much money as possible. In his *Advice to a Young Tradesman* he drummed away at this theme: "Remember that time is money. . . . credit is money. . . . money can beget money."

It was only a short step from this sort of thinking to our present, totally distorted view that the calling is merely a career, even if it's a career that God somehow guides us to. Or as Professor Fullerton put it, "Capitalism saw the business significance of calling, removed the transcendental, other-worldly motive, and transformed 'calling' into a job."

In part, these historical developments explain the present fix we're in. People believe that God—or the ultimate meaning for their lives—somehow is involved in their careers and work lives. Yet at the same time, they have bought into a limited, materialistic, distorted notion of the calling, a notion that is the antithesis of anything God apparently has wanted for His children.

He doesn't want us to pursue money for its own sake. He wants us to follow *Him* for *His* sake. He doesn't want us to make worldly success or achievement our number-one priority. He wants us, instead, to put our love for Him first and our love for others second. Only after we have these priorities in place are we ready to consider the role of achievement and success in our lives.

Unfortunately, though, we've managed to get everything backward. Success has crept up to first place, and everything else, including God and other people, has been integrated and organized under this top priority—this god, this idol.

But our lives are not integrated at all under the domination of this Success Cult. They are fragmented, confused, and frustrated. So that you can understand better why all this is so, in the next few pages we'll consider how this contemporary success "religion" is structured and how it has managed to lure so many into its clutches.

WHAT IS THE AMERICAN SUCCESS CULT?

Probably the best way for me to describe the American Success Cult is to begin with a personal confession. Quite recently, I was a card-carrying member of the Cult. Fortunately, however, I finally realized the insidious nature of what had trapped me and, in many respects, was destroying my life.

The crucial moment occurred when I was counseling a woman in my office. All of a sudden, I started getting a general feeling of discomfort. Then without warning, a sharp pain hit my chest and my left arm. I broke out into a cold sweat, and I knew immediately, without doubt, that something serious was going on inside my body.

I couldn't focus on what the woman in front of me was saying. So I decided I'd better terminate the session and take swift steps to find out what was wrong. When she had left the room, I hurried from our pastoral offices at St. George's Episcopal Church in Manhattan and headed directly to the emergency room in a nearby hospital. The medical staff checked me in, wired me up to an electrocardiogram machine, and eventually moved me upstairs to a cardiac care unit, where I stayed for four or five days of tests.

At first, the doctors had some trouble identifying exactly what was wrong with me. Obviously, they were concerned that I might have had some sort of heart attack. Heart problems run in my family, and physically I was a relatively high risk. I had been laboring under considerable tension, and I was fatigued and overweight.

Finally, at the end of the series of tests, the doctors determined—to my great relief—that I didn't have a heart condition. Instead, they said, I was suffering from severe gastritis, or considerable upset and discomfort in the upper part of my stomach.

I soon realized that the key thing was not the precise nature of my physical problem. While I was resting in the hospital and undergoing the tests, I had plenty of time to reflect seriously on how my life had begun to get out of control. Among other things, I was constantly feeling frustrated because I couldn't do everything I wanted to do. I always took on too many responsibilities, and I'd regularly become anxious because I wouldn't be able to meet deadlines or live up to the standards I had set for myself.

As I considered what had been happening in my life, it became clear that I wasn't managing my schedule very well. I had allowed my basic priorities in life to get out of order. It's easy for someone in the ministry to assume that he can never do enough to help others or serve the higher interests of the community or society, no matter how much of a toll the effort may take on him as an individual or on his family.

This problem is not limited to conscientious ministers, priests, or rabbis. I've known many executives and professional people who have the same attitude toward their jobs. They feel that their work is the most important thing in the world for them. They sense a kind of mission, which must supersede all other activities, interests, and relationships.

But whether you're a minister, a business executive, or any other type of worker, this kind of thinking is totally fallacious. Not only that, such a mind-set is virtually certain to get you locked into the insidious shackles of the Success Cult.

Fortunately for me, I had a clear-cut signal about the undesirable direction my life had taken, a signal short of death or other tragedy. Typically, though, those who are entrapped by the Success Cult will blithely continue to follow the way of excessive work and obsession with achievement until something in their lives explodes or falls apart. The temporary fame, power, or financial benefits of the Success Cult may be seductive, but the ultimate end is always dissatisfaction, personal difficulties, and sometimes outright disaster.

Some of the classic signs that the American Success Cult has thoroughly ravaged a person's life include a broken marriage, damaged health, a radical realization that one's life lacks ultimate meaning, or even sudden death.

I'm reminded, for example, of an article in the *New York Times Magazine* entitled "Hard Ball on Wall Street."[1] According to that account, a financially successful young investment banker had almost reached the top of his field. Certainly, he had most of the trappings of top-level success, including annual earnings that exceeded $350,000 and a home he had recently bought for $750,000.

But the emotional price had been high. He was in the process of working through a divorce with his wife, from whom he had been separated for two and a half years. The investment expert told the *Times* reporter that his marriage, at least in part, had been a casualty of the punishing hours he had put in on the job. Speaking of his marriage, he said, "I can look you in the eye and tell you that if I'd put more time into it, I probably wouldn't be where I am today."

Although I'd had several signals over the years that I might be caught up in the Success Cult, the latest and most frightening was the gastritis problem that put me in the hospital. Fortunately, my attack wasn't an unmitigated disaster. In fact, I really felt thankful because the incident made me re-evaluate and reorder my life.

For one thing, I resolved to exercise more than I'd been doing, and I got my weight down to a healthier level. Above all, I began to pace myself better.

I realized that "doing God's work" wouldn't, in itself, protect me from the subtle but personally damaging and potentially lethal impact of the Success Cult. Rather, on a regular basis, I had to delve down deep inside myself and pray, "God, show me how I can organize my schedule so that I can serve You effectively. Show me how I should establish my priorities in life. Show me how I can organize my schedule so as to make the best use of the mind, body, time, and opportunities You've given me."

By evaluating each item as it appeared on my daily schedule, I found that I could slow down the excessive speed of and involvements in my life. That way I was able to pace myself better through each day's activities.

For example, it's very difficult for reasonably sensitive, committed pastors to limit themselves when it comes to hospital visitations. Before my experience as a patient in the hospital, I would hurry from my administrative duties to my hospital visits, and then I'd rush from one patient to the next, devoting as much time as I possibly could to each individual.

I might visit one person who had a serious brain tumor and then another individual with a different terminal illness. The sessions could get extremely intense emotionally as I prayed and counseled, counseled and prayed. I'd typically stay with some families for an hour or two, with absolutely no time for rest, in part because I'd be standing up, engaging in unrelieved conversation during most of the encounters.

What I had failed to realize in the past was that an hour or two of such pastoral work was so demanding that it drained tremendous amounts of my energy. As a result, I really had little to give to my family or anyone else when I finished a day of hospital rounds. Eventually, the days, weeks, and months of the emotional toll of pastoral work, added to the administrative duties of being the rector of a large New York City church, caught up with me. That's the sort of thing to be expected when life is orchestrated by the standards of the Success Cult rather than by a more valid, balanced set of priorities.

But now, in more specific terms, what is this American Success Cult, which can devastate a person's health, marriage, family life, and spiritual well-being?

As I've evaluated my own experience, as a member of the Episcopal clergy and also as a friend and confidant of many high achievers in the business and professional worlds, I've come up with a more complete picture of this phenomenon. And make no mistake, what we're talking about here *is* a cult. As we've already seen, a cult by most classic definitions consists of

- cult leaders, who claim a complete corner on the truth;
- cult members, who receive intense indoctrination and constant supervision—a kind of "brainwashing" that allows for no understanding of reality other than that promoted by the cult; and
- cult values, which encroach upon and compromise orthodox doctrines and expressions of traditional religions, especially Christianity and Judaism.

As I've pondered this subject, I've been impressed with how much the American Success Cult resembles a distorted, off-center religious faith. First of all, like other cults, the Success Cult has moved into a vacuum created by the spiritual and moral bankruptcy of traditional religion. Our current religious institutions often lack real spiritual vitality. As a result, many average, reasonably intelligent people, including a great number of young executives and professionals in their twenties and thirties, have become disillusioned with traditional religion. They take one look at what's going on in many of our churches and synagogues and conclude that there's absolutely nothing there to attract them.

In general, we've lost our moorings of spiritual authority, our belief in the supernatural, and our understanding of how to find God's will in this world. Too often, many traditional religious groups have become nothing more than another variety of nonprofit institution. They lack the resources to respond to lay people who are looking for answers to the deepest questions of life: Is there a God? Who is Jesus Christ? Can God have a personal impact on my life today?

Our churches and church leaders often don't deal with these fundamental questions. Instead, they play around the edges by relying on irrelevant issues or detached social statements without a firm spiritual basis. Many of our seminary graduates and seasoned religious leaders lack an understanding of such spiritual basics as prayer or biblical morality. Furthermore, these leaders sometimes know little about expressing authentic love and servanthood toward others.

The Success Cult, in contrast, provides what seems to many to be a legitimate set of answers to the meaning of life. Also, the tantalizing fringe benefits of the Cult, including big money and a garden of hedonistic delights, may appear to be a preferable and far more delectable substitute for the sterner values and pie-in-the-sky heavenly rewards often associated with true faith.

But the quasi-religious offerings of the Success Cult don't stop here. An entire set of doctrines, liturgies, and faith practices may accompany this materialistic faith. I've identified a few Success Cult beliefs and practices, and grouped them into more-or-less related categories, beginning with conversion and moving through various stages of pseudospiritual experience.

CALLED INTO THE CULT

Conversion

For the Success Cult, the born-again experience involves turning *away* from many of the fragmented values of youth and turning *toward* the single, integrated goal of temporal success. Those who make this commitment consciously decide that they want to achieve as much as possible in their chosen field. At the same time, they acknowledge they want to gain as much power, status, and money as possible.

Before conversion, you may not have quite settled on what you want to do with your life. After conversion, you possess more of a single focus as you begin to climb up the ladder in your particular occupation.

The Calling

At the same time you're converted, you feel called by the demands of secular culture to enter a particular field and rise as rapidly as possible to the top. Whereas traditional Christians may feel called to a life of commitment to Jesus Christ, those enmeshed in the Success Cult are called to more temporal, materialistic goals and aspirations.

THE SACRAMENTS OF SUCCESS

In Christianity, a *sacrament* is sometimes defined as "an outward sign of God's inner grace." In the Success Cult, a sacrament might better be described as "an outward sign of outward achievement." Here, then, are five of the seven traditional Christian sacraments turned inside out to meet the requirements of the Cult.

Baptism

Baptism is a rite of passage that introduces the individual to his new faith and serves as a symbol of "dying" to the old life and being "resurrected" into the new life. For the authentic Christian, baptism carries a deeply mystical, eternal meaning. But for someone primarily driven by the tenets of the Success Cult, baptism becomes more a rite of passage into a chosen field.

For example, you could be "baptized" into your new profession on your first day at work simply by being exposed to the demands of your new occupation. Or you may experience a kind of baptism during the graduation exercises from a business school. Or this success sacrament may occur during a special celebration involving family or friends to mark the new era that is about to begin in your life.

I can remember one stockbroker who, on one of his first days at work, visited the floor of the New York Stock Exchange. "That truly was almost a mystical experience for me," he said. "The excitement and action occurring all around made me aware, in a way that I had never felt before, that I was definitely in the right place. I was exactly where I wanted to be for the foreseeable future."

The Eucharist

The Eucharist (also called Communion, Holy Communion, or the Lord's Supper) has long been a major sacrament or ordinance of the Christian church. The term *eucharist* comes from a Greek word meaning "the giving of thanks or gratitude." The sacrament was originally intended as a means for human beings to express their thanks to God for offering His Son as a sacrifice for their sins. Hence, the wine of the Lord's Supper represents Christ's blood, and the bread or the wafer represents His broken body.

But another kind of eucharist has developed in our modern-day working world. Testimonial dinners in various corporations around the country have taken on the trappings of great eucharistic feasts. At these gatherings, which often occur at the nation's great banquet halls and hotels, hundreds or even thousands of executives and other luminaries give thanks to corporate leaders and other highly accomplished stars who have made great contributions to their company, community, or society. Such events are great celebrations, great liturgical happenings, which enhance the influence of the Success Cult.

Those attending often pay hundreds or even thousands of dollars for the privilege. Then after the bills for the food and other expenses have been paid, the money that's left over—or perhaps I should say the "crumbs that fall from the table"—may be given to a charitable organization. Generally speaking, though, the great bulk of the money at these events is spent on wining and dining the elite and paying for the rental of the banquet hall.

Smaller eucharistic celebrations and feasts for the Cult may occur when executives go out for business lunches. They may spend an hour or more breaking bread together, patting themselves on their backs, and chatting about their plans and hopes for the company's future direction.

Confirmation

In the Christian tradition, a denomination may schedule confirmation when a young person becomes a teenager. At that point, the purpose is to instruct the youth so that he understands the true meaning of his baptism, which occurred during infancy. In this way, the adolescent is supposed to be placed in a position to move ahead in his relationship with God by developing a more mature, independent faith.

Of course, many young teenagers simply aren't ready for this step. As a result, some traditions emphasize a "spiritual confirmation" whereby an older person, often an adult, will recognize the need to make an independent commitment to Christ.

For the Success Cult, there is a similar kind of sacramental experience. Even after a person is "converted" and "baptized" into the fast-track life of ambition, superachievement, and upward mobility, there may still be some doubts. The commitment may be more tentative than permanent. The young achiever may think, *Well, I'm going to try this awhile and see how I like it. But I'll certainly switch to another field or try something else if this doesn't work out.*

Usually about five years into the experience, the initial commitment and baptism will be "confirmed" by early promotion, special affirmations and encouragement by superiors, or perhaps recognition by the outside world. I sometimes think the most powerful kind of confirmation for a business person—one that almost always assures that the individual is far along on the success track—is to be written up in the business section of the *New York Times*, the *Wall Street Journal*, or *Fortune* magazine. When you make it into one of these publications, you've "arrived," at least in some sense. You're now a solid member of the faith.

Ordination

Those who are destined to become leaders in the Success Cult always go through a kind of "ordination" in that they are selected by those more experienced in the "faith" to carry on the traditions into the future. For many people, this ordination first occurs when they are promoted to a particular level of management or expertise. For attorneys, for example, ordination may involve moving from the level of associate in a law firm to the position of full-fledged partner.

Also, there may be subsequent levels of ordination as individuals move up in the hierarchy. Going from junior to senior management is a big step in many corporations. In some ways, this may be the equivalent of moving from the level of pastor to bishop or from bishop to archbishop.

Marriage

Sages in every historical era have understood that the gifted, successful person in any field often becomes "married" to his work. For instance, in his 1860 essay, *Conduct of Life*, Ralph Waldo Emerson wrote: "Art is a jealous mistress, and, if a man have a genius for painting, poetry, music, architecture, or philosophy, he makes a bad husband, and an ill-provider."

In a similar vein, when the great nineteenth-century U.S. Supreme Court Justice Joseph Story became a Harvard Law School professor, he declared, "I will not say with Lord Hale that 'The law will admit of no rival, and nothing to go even with it'; but I will say that it is a jealous mistress, and requires a long and constant courtship. It is not to be won by trifling favors, but by lavish homage."

And what about the high achiever's *real* marriage? Too often, it will fall apart under the stresses and strains of hard, demanding occupational effort. If that doesn't happen, the husband-wife relationship will surely take second place to the worker's first love, which usually involves top-level professional achievement and plenty of power, money, and public recognition for a job well done.

WORKING OUT YOUR SALVATION

Salvation

Paul has told us, "For by grace you have been saved through faith, and that not of yourselves; it is the gift of God, not of works, lest anyone should boast."[2]

With the Success Cult, it's just the opposite. Salvation is by works rather than by grace. In other words, you have to work your way into the "heaven" of high achievement; you can't rely on the mercy and grace of your superiors. That old-time gospel hymn "Just As I Am," which says God accepts us with all our shortcomings, doesn't apply in the Success Cult. Your boss certainly won't accept you just as you are. You have to prove your mettle to him.

Also, salvation by the standards of the Success Cult is in many respects thoroughly unattainable. For one thing, what does it really mean to be "saved" by success? For many people, the answer goes something like this: I expect to be financially secure . . . respected

by the rest of the community . . . so powerful that I
don't have to be accountable to anyone . . . anchored
internally by a strong sense that my life has had a major impact.

But these goals usually remain beyond reach. Financial security is threatened when a major company
goes out of business or the national economy runs
into trouble. Status and power disappear for almost
everyone at retirement, if not before. And I've never
met anyone who experienced a permanent sense of
meaning and purpose in life as a result of what was
accomplished at work. No matter how much acclaim
you receive or how high you may go in a given organization, something is always missing.

The Great Commandment

Jesus said the "great commandment" is this: "You
shall love the LORD your God with all your heart, with
all your soul, and with all your mind."[3] But the Success Cult commandment might be stated this way:
Don't ask why you should take a given action or what
the moral implications of that action are. Just ask how
you can do your job better and more efficiently.

Actually, this statement paraphrases the basic ethic
of the Nazi management expert Albert Speer. He never
questioned the ultimate goals toward which his
actions were taking him. He just accepted the Nazi
cause as a given and served his master, Adolf Hitler,
without question or reservation.

In the Success Cult, a corollary to this great commandment is that you're supposed to do your best,
reach your maximum personal potential, rise as far as
possible in your chosen field, and contribute signifi-

cantly to the financial well-being and reputation of
your organization. Because there is a dearth of absolute values in the Success Cult, someone deeply enmeshed in it may feel that any ideas, strategies, or
practices are acceptable, so long as they turn a bigger
profit. Also, if you happen to be skirting the edge of
the law—or perhaps going over the edge—that's okay,
just so long as you don't get caught.

The Scriptures

In our achievement-oriented society, there are many
"bibles," but in general they can be lumped under the
basic umbrella of the professional journals and books.
For physicians, the bibles would be the *New England
Journal of Medicine* and the *Journal of the American
Medical Association.* For business people, the scriptures might be the *Wall Street Journal,* the business
section of the *New York Times, Fortune* magazine, and
a variety of technical journals and management
books.

These sources give us our basic values and strategies for succeeding in life. Only rarely do those who
rely on these "success scriptures" read them in light
of the moral principles and spiritual precepts found in
the real Bible.

Sacrifice

For those who are really serious about achieving big
goals and making big money, the Success Cult requires various kinds of sacrifice. Certainly, children
and spouses must rate a lower priority than responsibilities at work. If you have to work late to finish a
project, then so be it. Those extra hours may mean giving up time playing with your son or daughter or

spending some quiet, intimate hours with your spouse. But that's the name of the achievement game!

One ambitious young corporate executive told me, "I feel free to work hard, long hours now because I'm not married. But when I get married—and especially when I have children—I've already made up my mind to give them the first shot at my time, even if that means giving up extra money or promotions."

That's a mature and commendable attitude. But I always wonder when I'm talking to such a young person whether these lofty aspirations will hold up later when hard choices have to be made. Once you get into the habit of marching to the cadence of success and putting in those long, demanding hours at the office, it's very difficult to backtrack. You may have a spouse who needs your presence or a child who is experiencing a vacuum in his development because Mom or Dad isn't around. Yet changing your deeply ingrained priorities and achievement habits can be very, very difficult.

Sometimes, when I think of the sacrifices required by the Success Cult, I'm reminded of the biblical accounts of the worship of Molech, the god of the Ammonites. This ancient deity required the sacrifice of children by fire.[4] According to the Mosaic law, anyone who sacrificed his child to Molech was subject to the death penalty. In our own day, however, such sacrifice, while not by fire, often is the occasion of praise from the Cult hierarchy. After all, putting the job first and the family second reflects total commitment to the demands of the job.

Many times, those involved in the Success Cult are oblivious to the pressures and hardships they're plac-

ing on their families. Ironically, success would often
be impossible without the "back-up troops," including spouses who keep the household running and the
children functioning so that domestic concerns don't
get in the way of careers.

I'm reminded of a prominent clergyman who was
being honored at a party by various civic, business,
and religious leaders. One bestower of praise walked
over to the honoree's wife and asked, "What does it
feel like to be married to a saint?"

"I don't know—ask my husband!" the wife shot
back.

Much of the work of the Success Cult is made possible only because of the sacrifices, including the broken bodies and spirits, of spouses and children who
have been deprived and brutalized in the achievement
process.

Fellowship

In the New Testament, the Greek word frequently
translated "fellowship" is *koinonia*, a term that encompasses community sharing, encouragement, and
mutual edification among believers. There's a similar
fellowship in the Success Cult, but those participating
usually feel considerably more limited in what they
can say than do those in a genuine religious fellowship.

In general, there's a lack of true intimacy in business and professional relationships because coworkers often have mixed motives in their relationships. Those on the same level are usually competing
for promotions, awards, or recognition. So if you let
down your guard too often, you may find yourself get-

ting undercut or stabbed in the back by individuals you had hoped would help you. If you let your boss know your weaknesses, you may find that he's sympathetic on one level, but on another level, he may be less willing to give you the nod over someone else when he's ready to pass out promotions or other special considerations.

Any display of weakness is a real liability for you if you wish to be fully accepted in the Success Cult. Also, if you get too wrapped up in the personal concerns of colleagues or subordinates, you're apt to lose sight of your ultimate, overriding goal, which is loyalty to your organization and its potential for high cash flow and other signs of success.

I can recall one executive who was in charge of planning moves to other parts of the country for various junior people. He said that he was reluctant to get too friendly with any of them because if he did, they might be tempted to put excessive pressure on him. For example, they might ask him to delay their moves or encourage him to move them to certain locations that might be good for them but not so good for the company.

This man's primary concern was what was good for the organization and not necessarily what was good for the individual. In fact, he defined the individual's good *only* in terms of the company's good. In such an atmosphere, there may be an outward form of fellowship and intimacy, but the form may be largely devoid of substance.

WHAT DOES THE SUCCESS CULT
SAY ABOUT SIN?

The Day of Atonement

In the Jewish tradition, the Day of Atonement, or Yom Kippur, is the most important holy day. No one is supposed to work; everyone must fast; and God is asked to forgive the people of all their sins and broken vows. In ancient times, Israel's high priest took blood from a sacrificed he-goat into the Holy of Holies, the most sacred inner sanctum of the temple or tabernacle. There, he sprinkled it about to atone for the sins of the people.

I often think of the corporate annual meeting as the Success Cult's "day of atonement." At that time, the chief executive officer (CEO) stands up and fields questions from shareholders, and often from the press, about the company's performance during the past year. Also, he makes projections about what he expects of the future profit picture and corporate strategies. If the CEO and his cohorts have failed to live up to expectations during the last year, he'll certainly have to atone for their sins.

The Unforgivable Sin

In the New Testament, the unforgivable sin is blasphemy against the Holy Spirit. But I've discovered that in polite, upscale urban society, you commit the unforgivable sin when you start talking seriously about Jesus Christ. Whenever I say, "Let me describe in a little more detail what my experience with Christ means to me," I get a rather predictable reaction from those enmeshed in the Success Cult: glazed eyes, vague discomfort, and an obvious desire to change the subject.

On the other hand, individuals at even the most respectable dinner parties are willing to consider seriously much more incredible notions if they think there's some chance such notions may improve their lives. For example, the practices of various Eastern cults, which purport to give peace of mind and serenity, are often popular topics of conversation, primarily because they offer a quick emotional fix at little cost of time, energy, or commitment. I'm sometimes amazed to hear otherwise traditional, staid moguls of industry or society matrons discussing how certain psychic concepts, weird management philosophies, or even astrology may be the key to greater productivity.

The unforgivable sin in our success-obsessed culture is to reject these offbeat ideas and to affirm the power and authority of the God of the Old and New Testaments, who is not primarily concerned with productivity. Instead, this true God demands a life of love and servanthood, a life that may lead not to worldly achievement and success, but to rejection and the Cross.

Apostates

Apostates, of course, are those who reject the true faith. In the Success Cult, an apostate would be someone who says, in effect, "I'm not going to go along with these distorted, achievement-obsessed rules and standards that everyone else is following."

One couple I know made a startling choice for a pair of classic yuppies (young urban professionals). The young woman, who was in her late twenties, had been doing quite well in a major urban law firm. If she continued to demonstrate her high level of commitment and work the long hours she had been putting in, it seemed almost certain she would become a partner in her firm in a few years.

Her husband was on a similar fast track. As a highly successful executive in a major brokerage firm, he also worked late most days of the week. But his effort and commitment were paying impressive dividends in terms of high pay and great prospects for future promotions. Between them this young husband and wife were making more than $400,000 a year in income, and they could afford anything they wanted in the way of material goods.

However, all was not well in their multiroom penthouse cooperative apartment or in their sprawling beachfront weekend home in the Hamptons on Long Island. For one thing, both realized that they had been working too hard. They had been shortchanging their relationship as well as other values they held dear, such as their friendships and their church commitments. Not only that, the young woman had just discovered that she was pregnant.

So they were faced with some difficult choices. The thought of abortion crossed their minds, but both were morally opposed to it. Still they wondered: *How can we bring a child into this hectic, frenetic world that we've created for ourselves? We rarely spend any time at home together!*

Their answer: *We're going to change our world!*

In short, this young husband and wife decided to go against the grain of materialistic standards, distorted achievement, and unbridled ambition, which had entrapped them in the past. The wife decided to risk not being made a partner in her law firm. The husband began to see fewer clients and in general cut his business commitments back considerably.

The professional repercussions of these decisions remain to be seen. But there's been a tremendous transformation in this couple's family life. First of all, they have gotten to know each other much better. Also, they're enjoying their lives together in ways that had been impossible when they were both so deeply mired in their careers. Finally, their young son has just been born, and both parents are enjoying the opportunity of building a relationship with him.

These two have become apostates, former true believers who now reject the standards of the Success Cult. They are now pursuing more significant and enduring human and spiritual values.

Excommunication

Excommunication is a rare thing in the church and usually occurs only after the most outrageous rebellion or sinful conduct. Although many committed to the Success Cult don't know it, excommunication is a very common thing in the world of work.

The simplest, most direct form of excommunication is getting fired. I know one highly competent manager in his early fifties who had worked for many years in a major corporation. The particular company had developed the reputation over the years of being a warm, employee-oriented place; a person who took a job there could count on a secure place to stay for his entire career.

But the national economy took a nose-dive, and the corporation also fell on hard times. As a result, the top executives in the firm began a series of layoffs, and finally, my friend, like many of his colleagues, got the ax.

"What did I do wrong?" he asked his immediate superior, who had been given the task of conveying the bad news.

"Nothing," his boss replied. "You didn't do a thing wrong. It's just the way things are right now. I may not have a job myself before long."

My friend discovered that his boss hadn't given him an accurate evaluation of the situation, though. Most of the people who were being laid off were relatively senior, highly paid middle managers. In other words, the company's executives had gone after him and others holding similar jobs because they knew they could save more money by cutting those with larger salaries. Those higher up on the corporate ladder decided that in light of the financial pressures, he just wasn't worth the money he was being paid. So they let him go.

At the present time, my friend has entered into a class action suit against the company, charging, among other things, that the firm has discriminated against older workers. Also, after an intense job search for several months, he has found a good job with another company and now makes a salary equivalent to what he was earning before.

Right now, this man seems headed toward a relatively happy ending to his career woes. But he has been confronted with devastating emotional turmoil and tremendous blows to his sense of self-esteem by the treatment he has received, and he's become somewhat wary and cynical.

"If I haven't learned anything else," he said, "I know now that for any business, when push comes to shove, profits always come before the needs of the individual. If you don't seem to be contributing what your bosses expect to those profits, you're going to be in danger of being thrown out into the street"— excommunicated.

Sometimes career excommunication occurs in more subtle ways. For example, one way to be given the message that you're being excommunicated is to be passed over for promotion. That's a rather clear sign that you're no longer on the fast track to the top, that you've been derailed.

One man, who had just turned fifty and was in a high level in his corporation, had a reputation of being a leading expert in marketing a certain type of men's apparel. He came into my office quite depressed one day and told me that he had been passed over for further promotion. "So I'm thinking about taking an early retirement. For me, it's basically all over now," he said.

"What do you mean it's all over?" I asked. "You're barely fifty years old! And besides, you've accomplished a great deal. You have a wealth of experience and expertise that you'd be wasting if you quit now."

"I mean it's all over because there's no possibility of moving ahead, and that means no possibility of moving into other interesting professional areas. So there's really no reason for me to stay in this company. If I don't stay here, where else can I go?"

As he talked, I almost had the sense that he could easily have added the phrase ". . . and no more reason to live." He had completely lost confidence in himself, all because he had allowed his personal identity and self-esteem to become excessively dependent on his superiors' evaluations of his performance.

"Have you checked to see whether other companies might be interested in you?" I asked.

"I've been with this company for twenty-five years," he replied. "I wouldn't know where to start. Besides, I have some pension money, and I've managed to invest my savings rather well. The kids are finished with their schooling, so our expenses aren't that bad. I think maybe the time has come to put myself out to pasture."

Although there's often nothing wrong with taking an early retirement, I couldn't abide the depressing images of himself that he was communicating to me. I knew he had plenty of money, but that wasn't the main issue. Having grown rather close to this man over a number of years, I realized, better than most of his acquaintances, that going from such an active life with so many responsibilities to being on a perpetual vacation probably wouldn't be good for his emotional or physical health.

We talked further, and he eventually agreed to check with a couple of executive search firms, just to see if there might be some interesting possibilities. Within six weeks he found himself in the unexpected position of having to weigh the relative merits of three job offers, two of which involved a larger salary than what he was presently earning!

He ended up taking one of the positions, and almost

overnight, he got a new lease on life. But the wonderful thing about this final resolution of his problem was not that he got a better job or more money. Rather, he came to realize that the ultimate meaning of his life didn't depend on only one particular job.

Another kind of excommunication can occur when a person retires. Executives who have risen quite high in their fields may have tremendous responsibilities and command great respect. But they lose it all the day they leave their jobs.

They've done nothing wrong. They haven't received any disapproval, such as being passed over or told they're not doing a good job. Yet there's a tremendous vacuum of power and status, which can be devastating for them.

The entrepreneur Warren Avis has noticed that many former executives die soon after their retirement. He notes that it's "not because of heart attacks, but because of broken hearts."

THE LANGUAGE OF SUCCESS

In addition to these quasi-religious characteristics of the American Success Cult, the Cult has borrowed religious language from various religious traditions. For example, I've frequently heard people from a variety of fields use the following terminology:

"He's the anointed one." *Interpretation*: He's the heir apparent, the "fair-haired boy," who will probably succeed to the boss's mantle.

In a big midwestern bank, for example, three men were vying for the position of CEO, and all had excellent qualifications. But only one, we'll call him Dave, was the current CEO's favorite. That gave him a tremendous advantage when the board of directors finally cast their votes, so he got the job.

One of the losers, who was mulling over his future at a subsequent social event, was philosophical about the outcome. "The decision had been made before the board even met," he said. "Dave was the guy who had already been anointed."

"I am God here." *Interpretation:* I'm the absolute boss and anything I say goes.

One top executive gave his subordinates considerable leeway in arguing their positions on different issues. But when all the points had been presented and he had finally made up his mind, the boss would state his decision and move on to the next topic. If they disagreed at that juncture, he might let them know in no uncertain terms who was in charge.

One time, after a particularly heated discussion with three of his top-level executives, he broke into the interchange, said he had made his decision, and then told them what it was.

"But that could really hurt our profit picture!" one of the disappointed participants protested.

"Well, that's what we're going to do," the boss replied tersely. "Now, let's move on."

"But don't you think we should . . ."

"Look!" the boss interrupted. "Who's God here? You or me?"

The answer was implied in the question. And if you're caught up in the Success Cult, you don't argue with the god who's running the show.

"We need a born-again approach to this." *Interpretation:* We need a new marketing strategy, product, or whatever to improve our profit picture.

One Madison Avenue advertising firm was willing to try almost anything to keep a major corporate client, an insurance company, that had been threatening to transfer their account to another agency. The president of the ad company called a meeting of the account executives, copywriters, and art directors.

"Okay," he announced. "I want you people to get some religion today. We *have* to keep this client, or some heads will roll around here. A substantial part of our income comes from this insurance company. So let's hear some new ideas and concepts. It's time to get *born again* with this client!"

The conversations that ensued resembled a revival meeting more than a business conference. The resulting enthusiasm and concentrated effort lasted well into the night, with the group sending out for food and canceling personal evening engagements. Finally, after all the work and time, they managed to come up with what they thought was a salable new concept.

Unfortunately, the story doesn't have a happy ending. The advertising firm did get a better reception from the client with their new born-again marketing strategy than they had with their previous proposals. But apparently, the insurance executives felt they needed new advertising blood. Ultimately, they went with a new agency.

"I feel important vibrations in this situation, almost like some sort of spiritual power. Let's check this out." *Interpretation:* I don't understand what's going on around here, and I think we'd better try to find someone who does.

Increasingly, the old-fashioned occult has crept into the executive suites of corporate America. Just recently, for example, the *New York Times* ran an article entitled "Psychics Meet Wall Street" in which William Flanagan, a senior editor of *Forbes* magazine, said: "Psychics pick up on the vibrations and energy levels coming from Wall Street—which is nothing to be sneezed at."[5]

The main thrust of the article was that a number of stockbrokers, investment bankers, and others who trade on our financial markets are consulting psychics who rely on crystal balls, tarot cards, and other occult paraphernalia. Many of those attending this particular session, which took place on an excursion cruise around Manhattan Island, refused to give their last names. The reason for the secrecy? As one businessman said, "I can't be identified as getting psychic opinions." Still, he and the others were more than willing to delve into the spirit world in order to enhance their chances for success.

"This idea is going to be our salvation." *Interpretation:* We're on the way to greater success and more significant cash flow.

I've heard people in so many occupational fields make this statement that it seems to have become a standard part of our success-and-achievement language. Especially when times are hard in a business, there's a tendency to look for the one idea, person, or solution that is going to put everything right again and ensure future profitability. Sometimes, to be sure, one idea or person can be the answer that everyone's been looking for. But more often, the solution that's supposed to be the salvation turns out to be less helpful than hoped or expected.

In this regard, I'm reminded of one of the nation's most creative business minds who came up with an idea several years ago that changed the face of a major industry. But then he sold out his interest and went into semi-retirement. Finally, thoroughly bored, he tried to come back with still another earth-shaking concept, but without the great initial success he had enjoyed earlier.

In the years that have followed, I can't count the number of times that he's told investors and business associates, "This idea is going to be our salvation." At best, the ideas have been only mildly profitable, and at worst, they've lost him a great deal of money. In every case, they've fallen short of that permanent satisfaction and salvation he seems so desperately to need.

"You're going to have to do penance for that mistake." *Interpretation:* You've really got to show the higher-ups that you're sorry because of the mistake you made, and you have to work even harder to demonstrate your worth to this company.

One high-ranking officer in a major retailing firm made some projections that turned out to be considerably off target about a new catalogue venture. He had anticipated that the response of the public to direct mail and space advertising would be much higher than the actual response. As a result, his company lost money on the venture. In fact, many felt that this flawed performance was directly responsible for the lower profit picture at the company's next public accounting period.

This executive, who had displayed an excellent track record up to this point, retained his job. However, the vice chairman of the company let him know quietly but clearly that the company could afford only one such mistake before some of his important responsibilities would be shifted to other managers.

"He's my rabbi." *Interpretation:* He's my mentor, my spiritual guide, who will help me live up to the standards of the Success Cult.

In many of the nation's largest newspapers, it's a generally accepted fact that reporters don't move up to the level of editor unless they have a "rabbi," or mentor, to pave the way for them. I can recall a recent informal luncheon with New York City journalists where the conversation shifted to what editor was serving as rabbi for which reporter. As a matter of protocol, a reporter with a rabbi would never identify his mentor as such. But most of his colleagues knew who in the upper echelons of the company was helping his career along. As it happened, the person identified as having the managing editor as his rabbi soon moved up to the level of assistant editor—a position that started him on his way upward in the newspaper management.

BREAKING THE BONDS
OF SUCCESS SEDUCTION

This brief overview of the inner workings of the American Success Cult suggests that we're dealing with a system of values and beliefs that are vying for our ultimate allegiance as human beings. We may give lip service to the fact that God is the only One who deserves this sort of priority in our lives. But by conscious or unconscious commitment to distorted values of success, we push God, our families, and our friendships out of the top places they deserve. At the same time, we substitute much more limited, materialistic goals at the top of our list of priorities—goals that go under the guise of "maximum potential," "achievement," and "success."

As I've already told you, I can speak with some authority on these matters because I've been there. To one degree or another, consciously or subconsciously, I've affirmed many of the values and beliefs that I just outlined. And I've slipped into this trap even after making a conscious commitment of my life to Jesus Christ and genuinely attempting to find God's will for my life.

The result for me seemed to be total disaster when I suffered those chest pains and landed in the hospital. But fortunately, my illness was only a preliminary signal that I was heading for trouble. Now it was up to me to respond appropriately by breaking free from some of the shackles of the Success Cult.

After my hospital confinement one of the first things I faced was the out-of-control pace of my professional life. For example, I no longer ran frenetically from one hospital patient's room to the next. Realizing that I was probably doing the patients and myself more harm than good by this kind of frenzied hospital visitation, I would spend as much time as necessary with one patient. Then I would give myself permission to take some time off—as much as an hour if the session had been particularly draining. I might just walk from the person's hospital room over to a local museum and contemplate the art work. I've learned that going into a museum like this is one of the most restful things I can do to recoup some of my emotional and spiritual energies and to collect my thoughts.

Also, I began to measure the cost of success more than I had in the past. Jesus, in one of His parables, said that a builder never builds a tower without first sitting down to count the cost.[6] By the same token, I found that I had to evaluate each step I was taking in my work, just to see what cost I was paying for achievement, advancement, or recognition.

By taking some time to evaluate my activities, one by one, I found that the hypnotic effect of the Success Cult and its power of seduction were broken for me. It's so easy to get swept up in the momentum of accepting extra responsibilities, duties, and honors that you can lose sight of the price you'll ultimately have to pay in terms of your health, peace of mind, and family relationships.

I knew I had finally found a better pace and rhythm of success in my life when I got a letter from the mayor of New York asking me to consider becoming a commissioner of landmarks, a rather prestigious position that would have fit in with my interests and background. That very same day, I wrote a letter back to him saying, "Thanks, but no."

If I had accepted the position, I would have been able to share in wielding considerable power over the city's real estate interests, but the trade-off was that I would have been required to attend special meetings until midnight or later, two or three evenings a week. Also, there would have been the added strain of dealing with attempted manipulations by various developers and other real estate representatives.

Such a position, though it was a sign of success, just wasn't appropriate for me. I would have become personally overloaded and would have gotten mired more deeply in the seductive quicksands of the American Success Cult.

Perhaps my personal "confessions"—and some of the descriptions of the beliefs and practices of the cultic faith—have given you some idea of how the Success Cult has trapped others. Take a look at yourself now. Are you a part of this Cult? To answer this question, move on to the next chapter for the American Success Cult quiz.

CHAPTER FOUR

ARE YOU PART OF THE CULT?

Up to this point, you've been reading in some detail about what the Success Cult is and how it has developed. But how about *you* and the Cult? Where do you stand? Are you a part of it?

To answer these questions, try the following quiz.

THE AMERICAN SUCCESS CULT QUIZ

Please think carefully about the following questions, and answer them honestly. Respond with a yes or a no as you really feel, not as you think you *should* feel. It may be helpful to take the test privately so that you can feel free to answer from the gut level, without sensing you have to put up a good front for a friend, spouse, or other family member.

_____ 1. Does your job interest you more than your nonworking personal relationships?

_____ 2. Do you spend at least half your waking hours each week at work, including commuting time? (Remember, there are a total of 168 hours in each week.)

_____ 3. Do you spend less than ten hours a week communi-

61

cating or actively interacting with your family members (excluding time spent watching television or engaging in other activities that preclude meaningful personal interaction)?

_____ 4. Do you have headaches one day a week or more often?

_____ 5. Do you periodically wake up with a start, perhaps with your head spinning or your stomach in knots?

_____ 6. Does your mind often seem to be going too fast or out of control?

_____ 7. Do you find you have little time for physical exercise?

_____ 8. Do you frequently have little time to eat or take a breather during the day?

_____ 9. Are you usually one of the last people in the office at the end of the day?

_____ 10. Do you have trouble falling asleep?

_____ 11. Do you plan on moving every few years to enhance your chances to get promotions?

_____ 12. Do you have fixed career goals that you want to achieve over the next five, ten, or fifteen years?

_____ 13. Have you formulated a strategy for improving your status in society?

_____ 14. Do you believe your spouse's main function is to support you in your efforts to achieve your career goals?

_____ 15. Do you think one of the best ways to show love is to give material gifts?

_____ 16. Is your personal identity mostly dependent on what job you have or on how much you achieve in it?

_____ 17. Is it important to you to reach the top in your field or in your volunteer activities?

_____ 18. Do you believe that, to a great extent, money can buy freedom?

_____ 19. Is it important for you to associate with famous, rich, or accomplished people?

_____ 20. Do you tend to choose your friends in large part on the basis of what they've accomplished in life?

_____ 21. Do you get frustrated, annoyed, or upset when there's not enough money available to buy something you want?

_____ 22. Do you tend to buy gourmet foods?

_____ 23. Is it important for you to have wine with most meals or an alcoholic drink before or after dinner?

_____ 24. Do you usually choose relatively expensive wines, beers, or other drinks?

_____ 25. Is it important to you to use cocaine or other illegal drugs regularly?

_____ 26. Do you usually buy designer clothes?

_____ 27. Do you avoid bargain stores, preferring instead to shop at boutiques or other upscale retailers?

_____ 28. Do you like the sense of being above the rules that apply to most people?

_____ 29. Would you like to rise to an occupational level where you don't have to be accountable to anyone except yourself?

_____ 30. Do you find it exciting to be given extra power or authority to exercise over others, whether in your job or in volunteer activities?

_____ 31. Do you feel more attractive sexually after you've achieved a new career plateau or reached some other long-sought-after goal?

_____ 32. Do you have fewer than two truly close friends, excluding your family members? (Close in this context means a person with whom you can share your most intimate thoughts and dreams and can enjoy mutual encouragement and support on a deep level. Don't assume that a person is a close friend just because you have known him or her for a long time or even because you see the person fairly regularly.)

_____ 33. Have you known at least two of your best friends for two years or less?

_____ 34. Have you been married more than once?

_____ 35. Do you feel your child's (children's) education is something your spouse should primarily be responsible for?

_____ 36. Do you assume your child's (children's) sports interests, music lessons, or other extra-school activities are something your spouse should handle?

_____ 37. Has it been more than a month since you advised or helped another person with his or her career or personal problems or goals?

_____ 38. Do you often find yourself wishing intensely that you can make enough money or rise high enough in your field so that your personal financial situation will never again be a concern?

_____ 39. Does it make you feel somewhat envious, jealous, or otherwise uncomfortable if someone else achieves a significant success?

_____ 40. Do you often find yourself measuring your level of achievement against what someone else has done?

_____ 41. Are you naturally a competitive person in your work, your personal relationships, or your leisure activities?

_____ 42. Do you sometimes wince inside when you realize that others in your high school, college, or graduate school class have risen to a more prestigious position or make more money than you?

_____ 43. Do you sometimes find it hard to congratulate a friend who gets a promotion or is recognized for some achievement?

_____ 44. When you first meet a new acquaintance, do you ask, in the first few moments of conversation, what he or she does for a living?

_____ 45. Complete this sentence: "I am _____." Did you fill in the blank with some career-related or work-related fact?

_____ 46. Is your identity as a person mostly tied up in your career identity? For example, do you have trouble imagining how to describe yourself other than in terms of your position at work?

_____ 47. Do you think your spouse or a close friend will in most cases first describe you as a person who holds a certain job?

_____ 48. Suppose you are an objective reporter writing your obituary today for a comprehensive newspaper article, and you have great latitude to write about your personal as well as your public life. Would you expect to include mostly your accomplishments at work or perhaps your achievements leading religious or volunteer causes?

_____ 49. Reflect on your life for a few moments. Would you say that your career and even your volunteer and religious activities have been more important than in-depth personal relationships?

_____ 50. Do you become self-conscious around people who drive more expensive cars or live in more expensive houses or apartments than you do?

_____ 51. Do you sometimes go to work even if you have a fever or are suffering from some relatively serious illness?

_____ 52. Do you think it's a good idea, perhaps a character-building attitude, for a person to "push through the pain" and keep on playing if he suffers injury on an athletic field?

_____ 53. Do you have any eating disorders, such as being overweight or suffering from anorexia nervosa or bulimia?

_____ 54. Is your religious life more or less "compartmentalized" in the sense that you pursue certain religious activities or commitments at specified times during the week, yet you don't allow this religious side of your life to affect your work or personal relationships?

_____ 55. Do you feel that prayer or faith in God is often a crutch for weak people?

_____ 56. Do you believe that it's relatively unimportant for a person, particularly a successful person, to believe in God?

_____ 57. Do you feel that spiritual pursuits, such as praying with fellow believers, attending Bible studies, or participating in worship, are largely a waste of time?

_____ 58. Do you believe that those who are generally designated as the "poor" or "oppressed" in our society should be left to work out their own problems, without any particular help from you or other relatively affluent individuals?

_____ 59. Do you feel that the most important part of your life is over now that you've been passed over for a job promotion?

_____ 60. Has a great deal of the zest gone out of your life now that you've retired?

_____ 61. In general, do you feel that the most important thing in life is doing your best?

_____ 62. If a person fails to get a promotion or live up to company expectations in executing some job assignment, are you inclined to regard that person as somewhat inferior or inadequate?

_____ 63. Do you feel it's relatively unimportant to tell another person about your deepest needs, feelings, or insecurities?

_____ 64. Have you broken a date with one (or more) of your children in order to meet some demand of your work or volunteer activities in the past two months?

_____ 65. Have you broken a date with your spouse during the past two months for the same reason?

_____ 66. Have you canceled your vacation or failed to go on vacation during the past twelve months because of the demands of your work?

_____ 67. Is it important for you to own or drive a fashionable car?

_____ 68. Is it important for you to live in a relatively exclusive location where other successful people are likely to live?

WHAT THE QUIZ MEANS

Any "yes" answers to questions in the quiz indicate that you are under the influence of the American Success Cult on a certain issue. "No" answers indicate you're *not* under the influence of the Cult on that particular issue.

So how do you stand overall in light of the answers you've given? The following scale should provide you with some idea:

8 Yes answers or fewer: You're largely free of the Cult.

9–18 Yes answers: You're under the influence of the Cult to some extent, but other values remain predominant in your life. Even if you're only a fellow traveler, it's important to take steps *now* to re-evaluate your personal standards, values, and habits.

19–32 Yes answers: You're a card-carrying member of the Success Cult, but you re-

	main at a relatively low level in terms of your involvement.
33–42 Yes answers:	You're a hard-core member and probably have been for some time. You can expect considerable difficulty in extricating yourself from the Cult.
43–51 Yes answers:	You're a leader in the Cult, and you probably exercise considerable influence over others in encouraging them to affirm distorted standards of success. There's still hope for you, but you have a significant vested interest in maintaining the standards and values of the Cult. So you'll probably have to reorder your life and priorities completely to escape.
52 Yes answers or more:	You're facing an emergency situation! Your well-being spiritually, emotionally, and physically, is in jeopardy. Seek help immediately from a qualified Christian counselor.

As you can see, the questions in the quiz have dealt with a variety of important personal issues:

- your relationship with your children
- your relationship with your spouse
- your basic priorities in life
- your physical health
- your emotional and spiritual well-being, including feelings of inner peace and satisfaction
- your attitude toward your material possessions

- possible substance abuse in your life
- the quality of your friendships
- your involvement in helping and serving others less fortunate than you

Generally speaking, persons who are involved in the American Success Cult score low marks in most of these areas. For example, in one recent group of studies reported in both *Psychology Today* and the *Wall Street Journal,* working mothers and fathers were shown to spend a shockingly small amount of quality time with their children. Apart from watching TV programs with the family, the dads spent only eight minutes a day interacting with their children in such intense, one-on-one activities as reading and personal conversation. The moms didn't do much better; they devoted only eleven minutes a day to such activities with their children.

The questions in the quiz have also been formulated to reflect some of the most serious problems associated with a distorted success ethic. Consider the following reports:

Women under pressure to succeed are manifesting an increasing incidence of eating disorders, smoking, drug abuse, and "other forms of self-destructive behavior," according to a report in the *New York Times.*[1] A variety of medical, psychological, and business experts interviewed in this study have concluded that many women "have found that juggling the jobs of wife, mother, social butterfly, and executive is more exhausting than exhilarating. They have lost control over their lives, and no prestigious business card can compensate for the loss."

The pressure is also on *pro football players.* They are

urged to "push through the pain" and play, even when they are injured. For the latest year in which the National Football League's injury statistics were analyzed, the study showed that injuries to players were up 20 percent over the previous year's rate.

One of the players, who typifies the decision to put success and performance above personal health, is a top safety for the San Francisco 49ers. He chose to have the smashed joint in his left little finger amputated rather than undergo surgery and risk missing any of the season's games![2]

Families of celebrities may develop a variety of difficulties as a result of success, according to an ongoing study at the Timberlawn Psychiatric Hospital in Dallas. The researchers, Dr. Harold Cronson, a psychiatrist, and Gary A. Mitchell, a family therapist, have found that the families of celebrities display a number of distinctive problems. These include social isolation, loneliness, an unbalanced sense of family responsibilities as the celebrity accepts few marital or parental duties, and unreasonably high expectations imposed on the children.[3]

The most successful people may get so wrapped up in their own projects that they start seeking dangerous outlets to relieve the pressure. In the process, they often overlook the simplest immediate needs of their families.

For example, the great baseball star Mickey Mantle relates in his autobiography, *The Mick* (New York: Doubleday, 1985), that he frequently got involved in heavy drinking bouts, which once caused his wife to lock him out, and another time resulted in an injury to her when he smashed up his car. Mantle says he was too preoccupied with his business ventures and now regrets not having spent more time with his children.

Success always brings with it a host of new problems, and no one is immune to this danger, not even *those in the arts.* In one survey of successful playwrights,[4] the writers indicated that the sudden wealth and celebrity status of succeeding with a play often led to self-doubt and conflicts about priorities in life.

Many of them agreed that "survival may be measured in dollars, but success is not." In fact, they tended to acknowledge, as the writer Christopher Morley once said, "There is only one success—to be able to spend your life in your own way."

A number of these writers had some difficulty balancing the need to make money with their desire to do the work that they really felt they should be doing. Many had problems placing the demand for interviews, lectures, and talk-show appearances in proper perspective so that they could meet some of these necessary demands of success and also set aside enough time to pursue their chosen work.

For example, when August Wilson was acclaimed for his play *Ma Rainey,* he recalled: "It was pleasing, but it was also hectic. There are so many distractions, everything from your insurance agent trying to sell you more insurance to invitations to local plays to legitimate business reasons for being away from home."

Also, the playwrights confronted serious emotional and spiritual demands. Marsha Norman, the author of *Night, Mother,* noted that "what happens during the moment of great success is that people begin to believe in you, place great faith in you, for no reason other than their need to believe. It's a terrifying moment. You know you're not worthy. You know you're destined to disappoint them. This is a particular problem in American culture."

Clearly, then, many successful people—in fact, probably *most* successful people—confront a variety of new and often unexpected challenges when they begin to achieve in a big way. It doesn't matter what field you're in; it doesn't matter how old you are; and often, it doesn't matter how stable your life has seemed up to that point.

Marching to the drumbeat of success and beginning to reap some of the rewards of achievement can subtly but inexorably turn your personal world upside down. The new challenges are often so overwhelming that they may put unbearable stresses and strains on your emotions and relationships. Specifically, you can expect difficulties with

- your inner peace;
- the stability of your family life;
- your physical and emotional health; and
- your basic sense of meaning and purpose in life.

These are the hard realities of the Success Cult, whose values and principles you may have knowingly or unwittingly affirmed. If you're in the Cult, or in danger of being pulled into its destructive orbit, what steps can you take to escape?

In the following pages of this book, we'll discuss in some detail ways you can reorder your life to protect yourself against the pervasive influence of distorted notions of success in our society. But first, just to start you thinking in the right direction, I'd like for you to do something that may seem to have absolutely nothing to do with success but actually has *everything* to do with it. I'd like for you to write your own obituary.

WRITE YOUR OWN OBITUARY

Many experts who have done research on the meaning of death—as well as the emotional problems of life—have suggested that it can be an informative and healing experience to write your own obituary. For example, Dr. J. William Worden, author of *P.D.A.— Personal Death and Awareness* (Englewood, N.J.: Prentice-Hall, 1976), conducted research on the subject of death and dying at the Harvard Medical School for more than a decade. Among other things, he advised those who were interested in exploring their own emotional problems, personal goals, or the meaning of life to sit down for a few moments to draft a personal obituary.

How can such obituary writing help with your approach to success? I've found that too often, as we get caught up in daily work pressures and the demands imposed on us by our society, we lose sight of where we're going. We forget our main purpose for living and our ultimate goals in life—if we ever had any in the first place! Writing your obituary can help you to stop for a few moments and evaluate where you've been in life and where you're headed.

So now, take out a clean sheet of paper and write your obituary following this format:

_____(Your name)_____ died suddenly yesterday. His (Her) greatest accomplishment in life was _____

_____.

   The most important things he (she) did for his (her) spouse were _____

_____.

   The most important things he (she) did for his (her) children were _____

_____.

   The most important thing he (she) did for his (her) other family members was _____

_____.

   _____(Your name)_____'s highest priority or main goal in life was _____

_____.

   He (She) worked toward that goal by _____

_____.

   On the last day of his (her) life, _____ (your name)_____ told a close friend that he (she) regretted not accomplishing, finishing, or doing the following: _____

_____.

   Obviously, there are no right or wrong answers for such an exercise. In writing my obituary, I discovered that I tended to focus not on the outward accomplishments of my life, but on the quality of my personal relationships, including my relationship with God.

   In fact, if I imagined myself at the end of my life right now, I'd have to say that the most important thing for me hasn't been any accolades, degrees, or public recognition of accomplishments. Rather, the really significant things have been the development of my ties with God and the nature of my interactions with my children and my wife.

   Yet when I ask myself how well I'm doing in nurturing those spiritual and personal relationships, I have to admit that I often fall short. The demands of daily work and the pressure to achieve or succeed always intrude. I must constantly remind myself to keep my eyes on Christ rather than on the earthly expectations that other people may have of me.

These are some of my personal conclusions and reflections as I've drafted my obituary. You'll have to reach deep inside yourself and come up with your own answers. But I expect that as you think seriously about these matters, you and I won't be too far apart in what we regard as ultimately important in our lives.

Up to this point, then, we've defined the problem with the American Success Cult, and we've discovered a few preliminary steps we can take away from the Cult. Now, let's explore what it takes to break completely free from this destructive system of beliefs and practices. Let's find out how we can achieve *true* success rather than this pale, distorted imitation that has been foisted on us.

C H A P T E R   F I V E

YOUR PERSONAL SEARCH
FOR TRUE SUCCESS

To break free of the Success Cult and avoid the danger of addiction to a distorted ambition, you must first of all focus on the positive—on what *true* success should be for you. Think about it for a moment: How do you define success?

I like to answer this question without referring to one-line definitions, which say succinctly but inadequately that "success is this" or "success is that." Instead, I prefer to explore the lives of people who, in some sense, seem to have been truly successful. Then I can build definitions from real life rather than from relatively meaningless abstractions.

In my life a person who has impressed me as embodying some of the best qualities of success is my friend Andrew Heiskell, former chairman of Time-Life, Inc. At one time it seemed that Heiskell's entire existence was consumed with overseeing the great Time-Life communications empire. So when the time arrived for him to retire a few years ago, many people wondered, How can this man survive when he leaves all that power and prestige behind? What can such a successful person do for an encore, except maybe get extremely frustrated, discontented, or depressed?

In many ways retirement is the acid test to determine whether or not a person is really successful. If all achievements have been work- or product-related, the transition from the accustomed world of work may be devastating. Furthermore, the person who can't make the transition isn't really quite so successful. And that's one of the things that has impressed me about Andrew Heiskell.

He didn't miss a beat after retirement as he continued to take on and overcome new challenges. In particular, he immediately assumed responsibility for upgrading the New York Public Library, a forbidding but extremely valuable and commendable objective.

Among other things Heiskell has embarked on a fund-raising drive to raise $300 million to endow the library, and he's well on his way toward achieving his goal. Also, he has taken a hands-on approach to dealing with the presence of drug pushers and loiterers in Bryant Park, which is adjacent to the main library building at Fifth Avenue and Forty-second Street in Manhattan.

Bryant Park is often called "needle park" because of the presence in the area of hypodermic needles used by drug users. Also, many of the homeless in the area gravitate toward the park and use the steps of the library as their "sitting room" and even as their bathroom. It's a place many ordinary citizens would prefer to avoid, but not Heiskell. When I've stopped by there on several occasions at lunchtime, I've seen him in the park checking things. He could easily petition for restricted access to the park but instead he's always evaluating how he can improve the situation and keep the library and the surrounding grounds open to everyone.

Because of the situation in Bryant Park, Heiskell has shown a particular interest in how our parish has been handling the problem of the homeless and the hungry in New York City. We have been sheltering about sixteen homeless people every night for many years, and we hand out six hundred free lunches each week to the hungry. Heiskell has had discussions with me, as well as with others, as he has formulated his strategies and policies for the library.

It's a tall order to revamp the deteriorating New York Public Library system. But it's a job I'm glad has been placed in the lap of Andrew Heiskell, a sensitive, responsible, and truly successful man.

Using Heiskell as a starting point, let me offer this tentative working definition of true success. As I see it, individuals who experience genuine success should

- demonstrate an ultimate allegiance to broader, higher values than values that just promote accolades or wealth for those individuals;
- achieve something of lasting value, though there may be no general consensus about what constitutes a great achievement or a lesser achievement;
- make significant use of their personal talents and gifts;
- demonstrate "staying power" in their chosen work, in the sense that they are able to stick with a job or responsibility, often for years, until that job has been finished; and
- perhaps be recognized publicly in some way for their work, such as by press coverage, promo-

tions, or monetary rewards—*except* they must always remember true success never depends ultimately on such recognition.

True success may involve the achievement of outward and even highly acclaimed goals, such as rising to high office, opening major new markets, writing widely read books, or otherwise gaining public recognition for one's accomplishments. At the same time there is also an *inner* dimension to genuine success—typically an interior strength, equanimity, and sense of direction without which the outer achievements will always seem to fall short or fail to satisfy.

SUCCESS STORIES

Certainly, in his work with Time-Life and with the New York Public Library, Andrew Heiskell seems to measure up to success by this preliminary definition. But I don't want to place on his shoulders or on anyone else's the burden of being the perfect human example of success. Rather, I prefer to draw from the experiences of a wide variety of men and women, many of whom I may not agree with on spiritual or other issues. That way I find I can piece together a more complete understanding of what it means to be a true success.

I've always marveled at the example set by St. Francis of Assisi, the thirteenth-century Christian ascetic who gave up a family fortune and a life of luxury to pursue his vision of God. After being told by God to rebuild the church of St. Damian, near Assisi in Italy, he sold his horse and some of his father's textiles. Then he turned over the money he received from the transactions to a priest for the construction of the church.

As a result of this radical act of philanthropy, Francis's father disowned him, but that didn't stop the young man. He went on to take a vow of poverty and also began to preach the gospel, with an emphasis on brotherly love and repentance for sins. Soon, other spiritually sensitive men began to follow him. The result was the establishment of the Franciscan friars and the beginning of a far-reaching tradition of religious orders and lay service that has influenced the Catholic and the Protestant movements to the present day.

But even as I hold up Francis of Assisi as a stirring example, I'm *not* saying that to be successful it's necessary to give away all your worldly possessions this moment and follow him in lock step. I know I haven't modeled my life, point for point, after his particular brand of asceticism or radical spirituality. It would be hard for anyone to meet his standards, and many people probably wouldn't want to approach life exactly as he did.

For example, according to the accounts of his life written by St. Bonaventure, St. Francis regularly observed seven canonical hours each day for his private prayers, and he always prayed, no matter what the circumstances. On one occasion, he was riding his horse in the country during a rainstorm, but the inclement weather didn't deter him when the time arrived for his prayers. He simply climbed down from his horse and, oblivious to the downpour that was drenching him, he finished his meditation. Then he continued his journey.

I don't know anyone these days who displays this kind of spiritual rigor, and for that matter, I'm not sure it's necessary for the average person to go this far with daily devotions. On the other hand, Francis's life has a lot to say to us about priorities. This medieval friar left a legacy that has lived on to the present day, yet he never pursued achievement only for achievement's sake. He always kept his primary goal of service to Christ and to his fellow man uppermost in his mind and at the cutting edge of his actions.

With his priorities in proper order, success and accomplishment by the world's standards followed naturally for Francis. He became famous and highly respected, even in his own day. Among other things Pope Honorius eventually recognized his work and gave his group an official designation as an order of the church.

Some other, more recent experiences of successful people have also been instructive for me, including modern-day businessmen, reformers, and even entertainment and sports figures. Again, I may not identify with the entire package of beliefs and the lifestyles that each person represents. But I do think they all have something important to show us about what true success involves.

The Social Reformers

In the 1960s and early 1970s, being socially and politically active was the popular thing to do for many people. Often without understanding the full implications of their actions, young and middle-aged people alike would turn their backs on the "establishment" and on traditional money-making occupations and would seek something "meaningful" to do for others.

The civil rights movement, antiwar movement, environmental movement, and other, lower-profile causes made considerable headway during those years. I became deeply involved in protesting racial bias, and I was arrested during one public demonstration. However, as the novelty and glamour of this sort of activism faded, most people seemed to focus on more parochial and self-centered concerns, such as getting attractive jobs and making a bundle of money.

Fortunately, even though the cultural climate has been less hospitable, some true reformers have managed to emerge. These deeply concerned individuals are willing to take risks with their future and their finances in order to promote certain worthy causes and help those on the lower end of the social and economic scale.

Those who have particularly impressed me in this regard are the ones who have left high-paying, upwardly mobile corporate and professional positions to work with the homeless. For example, a former member of my parish, Anne Troy, was one of New York City's top advertising copywriters, but she decided that she wanted to become more directly involved in helping others. In particular, she wanted to do the work of Christ among the poor and unfortunate.

So she quit her job and took a position that paid much less with the Habitat for Humanity program, the group that renovates tumbledown urban housing for use by the homeless and by others who can't afford regular city rents. Former U.S. President Jimmy

Carter has not only supported this program but has actually come to New York to do carpentry work.

Similarly, Robert M. Hayes, a former lawyer with the prestigious Sullivan & Cromwell firm in New York City, left his position to found the National Coalition for the Homeless, an advocacy group for the poor. Soon after he began this work, he was joined by Maria Foscarinis, also a lawyer with Sullivan & Cromwell. At this law firm, Foscarinis had been making a salary of $70,000 a year; with the coalition, she earned $10,000 in her first year. Nevertheless, she has managed to adjust by finding bargain prices for food, an automobile, and other material goods.

What motivates these new reformers to make such radical changes in their way of living? Foscarinis sums up some of the feelings this way: "Some people become involved in a movement for social justice because they themselves are discriminated against. But someone not in that group can also have real reasons for becoming involved. For me, it has to do with the kind of world I would like to live in."[1]

Are people like Anne Troy, Robert Hayes, and Maria Foscarinis successful? Of course they are, at least by many tests, except perhaps by the amount of money they make. Consider how they measure up to the standards we've tentatively laid down for true success:

- They seem to be motivated by an impulse higher than themselves—by God, by a deep concern for the welfare of others, or by both.
- They are taking significant steps to achieve great things for the underprivileged in our society.
- They are using their personal gifts in a big way.
- What they are doing has broad, lasting value.

- They seem to have plenty of personal staying power in their demanding pursuits.
- They often receive considerable recognition for their work.

But now, let's shift gears and take a look at the inner life of a man who has combined the skills of the super-investor with the generosity of the philanthropist.

The Investor-Philanthropist

John Templeton, the founder of the highly success-ful Templeton group of mutual funds, is widely recog-nized as one of the world's most successful investors and money managers. Listen to what some of the financial pundits have to say about him:

> **With his cool head and hand, he has produced a spectacular record. *Forbes,* which has inter-viewed them all, considers John Templeton to be one of the handful of true investment greats in a field crowded with mediocrity and bloated repu-tations.**
>
> **—*Forbes* magazine**

> **John Marks Templeton runs a fund whose high-flying performance defies gravity. There is probably no mutual fund that can match his Growth Fund for consistent superiority.**
>
> **—*Changing Times***

> **Templeton . . . is the most successful mutual fund manager of his generation. . . . He usually outshines the competition even more in bear markets than in bull ones.**
>
> **—*Money* magazine**

This quiet, modest, deeply religious man is one of the authentic heroes of Wall Street.
—Louis Rukeyser, columnist and host of the PBS program "Wall Street Week."

Despite his current stature and great renown on the world's money markets, Templeton didn't have success handed to him on a silver platter. He began in relatively humble circumstances, the son of parents of quite modest means in a tiny Tennessee town. In every way he has become a self-made man. He's found his personal route to great outward success, yet he has retained an apparently generous dose of inner tranquillity and satisfaction.

So what specifically has been the secret of Templeton's great success? In an authorized biography[2] and also in other interviews, he has revealed some inner "ingredients" that have led to his significant outward achievements.

Ingredient #1: Self-reliance. From early childhood Templeton was taught to think and act for himself. His parents would typically give him some initial advice and guidance, but then would leave him on his own to work out the details of different problems and projects for himself. As a result he developed a belief in himself, a deep sense of self-assurance and self-confidence.

Ingredient #2: Reasonable Risk Taking. Most successful investors—and Templeton is no exception—seem to have a bit of the entrepreneur in them. But Templeton isn't a wild gunslinger with other people's money. Rather, he moves carefully, and he thoroughly analyzes all the facts before he puts one penny on the line.

Ingredient #3: A Sense of Stewardship. As John Templeton has grown older, he has concluded that his money and great responsibilities for other people's wealth have been given to him by God. As a result he sees himself as a steward or manager of God's wealth.

One of the ways in which Templeton returns his money to others has been through the famous Templeton Foundation Program of Prizes for Progress in Religion. This prize carries a monetary award designed to be slightly higher than that of the Nobel Peace Prize.

The first winner of the Templeton prize was Mother Teresa of Calcutta in 1973. Since then many other religious luminaries have won, including evangelist Billy Graham; Cardinal Suenens, pioneer of the Roman Catholic charismatic renewal; writer Aleksandr Solzhenitsyn; and Sarvepalli Radhakrishnan, former president of India.

Ingredient #4: Flexibility. Like many other top investors, Templeton has general guidelines he follows, but he claims no ironclad formulas. He's always willing to roll with the punches when he confronts new situations and challenges. Consequently, when the stock market drops precipitously—as it did when the Dow Jones Industrial Average plunged more than 500 points on "Black Monday" of October 19, 1987—Templeton doesn't panic. Instead, when interviewed by journalists after that debacle, he noted coolly that he planned to go bargain hunting, even as other less experienced investors were selling wildly and generally losing their heads.

Ingredient #5: A Willingness to Spend Time Studying and Planning His Business Strategies. One of the keys to John Templeton's great success is that he doesn't waste a minute. For example, many people might regard as "dead time" the minutes or hours they spend waiting for or traveling on airplanes, and going to and from business appointments. In other words, they write the time off as lost.

But not Templeton. Instead of staring out into space, he peruses articles and studies by security analysts, or he catches up on some religious reading. As a result, he's one of the best-prepared investors in the world when it comes to knowing the facts about a particular opportunity.

Ingredient #6: An Ability to Retreat Periodically from Daily Pressures. The idea of the "retreat" is a religious concept that John Templeton has found to have direct application to his investment strategy. He moved from Wall Street to his present home in the Bahamas in the 1960s. From that time on, his success as an investor has improved markedly.

He has found that the hours he spends in solitude—including an hour or so each day on the beach, looking out over the clear green waters of Lyford Bay—rejuvenate him and inspire creativity. He says he gets a perspective during these times alone that is impossible to achieve in the turmoil of the New York financial markets.

Ingredient #7: An Extensive Network of Friends. A major characteristic of Templeton's personality is his ability to make and keep friends in a wide variety of places and businesses throughout the world. Of course, on one level, these friendships are important to Templeton entirely in themselves, without reference to what the people can contribute to his business. At the same time, however, many of these people hold influential positions in the business, investment, academic, and church communities. In these roles they can prove to be invaluable contacts when he's looking for information or advice.

Ingredient #8: Patience. One of the fruits of the Spirit cited in Paul's letter to the Galatians is patience.[3] As it happens, this spiritual virtue is also important in successful investing.

John Templeton has learned how essential patience is as he selects stocks and then waits calmly for them to start an upward climb. The wait may be months or years, but Templeton always takes the long view, and his patience has proved him right more often than not.

Ingredient #9: Mental Discipline. More than most people, Templeton has learned to focus his thinking so that he can concentrate on the task at hand and block out extraneous matters from his mind. He simply refuses to allow worries and anxieties unrelated to his work to intrude when he's honing in on a particular stock choice. He has achieved the ability, when necessary, to mass all his thinking and efforts on his work, resulting in his being considered one of the world's greatest investors.

Ingredient #10: Positive Thinking. As Templeton disciplines his mind, the main avenues into which he directs his thoughts involve positive subjects. He believes that negative thinking is a kind of psychological poison that saps a person's energy and distracts him from accomplishing important goals. Certainly, he recognizes and deals with poor investments when he encounters them, but he doesn't dwell on them. He moves on to investments that offer the promise of profit.

Ingredient #11: Trust in Intuition. As rational and analytical as Templeton can be, he always leaves room for the hunch, the inspired, intuitive insight. His intuition, though, generally comes from having laid a solid groundwork of facts and research.

For example, he predicted in the early 1980s, when the stock market's Dow Jones Industrials Index was below 1000, that the Dow could reach 3000 by the end of the 1980s. Although the Index has plunged far below that, the Dow hit an all-time high of more than 2700 in 1987.

How was he able to make such a remarkably close prediction years before the event occurred? In part, he relied on analyses of how investment money could become available from pension funds and other sources. But beyond these rational considerations, Templeton turned to his sense of intuition.

John Templeton, then, presents us with an unusual and inspiring picture of the inner bases of one man's outward success. A somewhat different, but highly instructive message comes across as we turn now to an actor who has been called an "American icon."

The American Icon
That's the way *Newsweek* described the popular actor, director, and film producer Clint Eastwood.[4] But

why an enduring cultural idol and not just some flash-in-the-pan celebrity?

Eastwood has made millions from his movies, and he has gained international fame for his roles in such films as *A Fistful of Dollars* and *Dirty Harry*. But just as significant as these outward, material signs of achievement is his staying power in his chosen field. Also, he's shown a degree of personal stability and an inner equilibrium, which count among the hallmarks of true success.

Many other people have made a few good movies or otherwise flirted temporarily with stardom. In a number of cases, though, they have either faded away or gone entirely off the track in their personal lives, such as with drugs, alcohol, or sexual immorality. To be sure, there's plenty of evidence that Eastwood isn't perfect. His marriage fell apart several years ago, and there are reports that he can be a hard taskmaster when he's making one of his films. But up to this point, Clint Eastwood has managed to maximize his talents and stay on the path that leads to true success.

Undergirding his achievements are several specific personal qualities, which have been noted by various observers of the film industry:

- He doesn't take himself too seriously, and he has the ability to laugh when things go wrong.
- He values loyalty to and from others.
- He doesn't play the prima donna when he's doing a movie; rather, he welds together a team and works for the most efficient completion of the film project.
- He works hard.

• He has the courage of his instincts and convictions.

As for this last point, Eastwood reportedly rejected the advice of those who warned him that his movie *Every Which Way but Loose* would fail because the public didn't want to see him in a funny role. In fact, their "scientific" market research showed the project was heading for disaster. But Clint Eastwood forged ahead and ended up with his most successful movie of all.

In each of these cases there is, to one degree or another, the linking of an inner and outer dimension of achievement that constitutes true success. Yet, even with the most successful people, an inner sense of well-being isn't always present. In a Gallup survey of people in Marquis's *Who's Who in America,* only 53 percent said they were "very happy"; 41 percent responded that they were "fairly happy."[5] Also, feelings of satisfaction, meaning, and "rightness" may be more complete for some successful people than for others.

I've found that top achievers always have some deep and stable spiritual belief, strength of character, or broad sense of perspective on life. Otherwise there can be no true success. A powerful position, money, and fame are simply not enough, by themselves, to make a person genuinely successful. Furthermore, the position-money-fame factors may so distort a person's view of personal achievement that he or she may fall victim to an addiction to success.

THE ADDICTIVE POWER OF POSITION, MONEY, AND FAME

When many people try to define success, the first thing that often comes to mind is rising to an important position or accomplishing some major task. Then there's the assumption that with a particular promotion or accomplishment, significant material rewards and recognition will follow.

So, a "successful" lawyer is, first of all, one who has risen to the highest level in a prestigious law firm or is a top performer in the courtroom. A "successful" business person is a senior corporate executive (preferably a chief executive officer) or an entrepreneur who has established a booming new business. A "successful" pro athlete is one who has demonstrated great skill in his sport and the ability to win consistently against his opponents.

Also, because our society often measures such achievement in monetary terms, the relative wealth of individuals may become the major test of success. Among the most fascinating journalistic events of the year are the reports on the finances of successful people, such as the annual publication of *Forbes* magazine's "four hundred richest people in America." These reports are so popular that the *New York Times*, the *Wall Street Journal*, and hundreds of other newspapers around the country dutifully report the *Forbes* findings every year.

Sam M. Walton, chairman and CEO of the Wal-Mart Stores, Inc., was the *Forbes* top banana in 1986, with a net worth of $2.8 billion. By the time the magazine was out, practically every newspaper and wire service in the country seemed to have the story. In another equally popular *Forbes* report on earnings by entertainers, Bill Cosby headed the list with an estimated $27 million in 1986 and $57 million in 1987.

Forbes is not the only publication interested in such titillating financial trivia. A study in *Financial World* magazine ranked the incomes of investment bankers and corporate takeover artists. This article noted that the number-one earner, Michel David-Weill of the Lazard Freres investment banking house, had pulled in a cool $125 million in 1986.

These are successful people—or are they? In responding to this question, you must be honest. Consider your *real* feelings, not just what you think you should feel. When you think about success, isn't the old dollar sign one of the first things that comes to your mind? After all, we've been conditioned to expect success to produce certain material benefits and rewards. One of my high-achieving friends once said to me, "What's the point of being successful if you can't cash in on it?"

For many people just being recognized for an accomplishment isn't enough. Or as one variation on the old saw goes, "With a certificate of achievement and fifty cents you can buy a cup of coffee!"

Why has money become such an important measurement of success? For one thing, it's an easy way to gauge relative achievements in many fields. People like to keep objective track of their success as compared with the success of others. To this end it's convenient to check your earnings against those of your competitors. If you make more money, you get more "points," and therefore, you're more successful.

Such ideas as being satisfied with your work or helping others or achieving a sense of personal worth are too hard to quantify if you're deeply involved in the success game. These goals are far too subjective and don't show you as clearly as money does how your accomplishments stack up against those of the other guy.

Money has become an important measure of success also because of what it can buy. In our materialistic society, a sense of personal security, status, self-esteem, and even the basic potential for happiness may seem to be wrapped up in an individual's buying power. We're bombarded from every direction with dollars-and-cents values. A headline in one recent supermarket tabloid, for instance, extolled "Dynasty's Real-Life Moneybags: George Hamilton owns more houses than the Carringtons—in fact, he's got one for sale at $6.5 million."[6]

Interest in such materialistic gossip is not limited to the low-brow lines of sensational journalism. The *Wall Street Journal* presented its version of the "Dynasty" TV ethic in a front-page feature entitled "Moneyed Atlantans Get Instant Status from 'Megahouses': New Homes Are Huge, Boast His-and-Her Everything; 'Dynasty' Bedroom Suites."[7]

Not to be outdone, the traditionally staid "gray lady" of newspapers, the *New York Times*, frequently reports on the lifestyles of the rich and famous, such as the movement among the moneyed to buy titles so they can become, for example, English lords of manors at an average $15,000 a clip.[8] Another frivolous but prominently positioned article in the *Times* business section focused on the art of selling to the very rich.[9] In glorious graphic detail, the paper pictured $75,000 crocodile luggage, a $2,970 silk suit-and-shirt combo, and a $1 million diamond wrist watch.

As a people we may say out of one side of our mouths, "I think such expenditures are downright scandalous! Such a focus on money is misplaced!" Yet we sing a different tune out of the other side. We whistle and "ooh" and "aah" when we hear of some extravagant purchase or financial achievement. And we continue to buy the papers and magazines that keep us up-to-date on the doings of the well-to-do. A couple of reports in major national publications, for instance, showed us how many millionaires there are in the United States (a million, by the most recent count). Also, we were told where those millionaires are most likely to live (measured by the ratio of millionaires to total residents, North Dakota is at the top, and West Virginia is at the bottom).

Broad personal notoriety, big bucks, and extravagant purchases provide the bottom-line definition of achievement for many people in our society. But is this really what true success is all about? Or is the extraordinary emphasis on material possessions simply a sign of the distortion of values that has been promoted by the American Success Cult?

True success turns out to be something quite different from the spangles, baubles, and skin-deep superficialities that sometimes pass for success. When asked by the Gallup organization how important they regarded some frequently mentioned "rewards" of success, a representative sample of real-life top achievers listed in Marquis's *Who's Who* responded in a rather unexpected way. They placed expensive belongings, social status, personal power, and unlimited money way down at the bottom. At the top, 80 percent of the achievers listed a "sense of personal worth and self-respect" as a "very important" reward of their success.[10]

An affirmation of values like a sense of personal worth and self-respect is precisely the point at which I would recommend that you too begin to build your definition of success. It's quite true that money, status, and power often follow in the wake of true success. But these outward, material signs of high achievement aren't the essence of it. People who strive primarily to acquire things, to increase their income, or to rise high in status and prestige will never really be completely successful.

True success, in contrast to the counterfeit, cultic, addictive version, involves inner growth and development more than outward acquisition and visible trappings. To put this another way, genuine success has a deep-rooted *staying power*. When you're a real success, you have a quality of inner strength, peace, confidence, and balance, which will stick with you indefinitely, no matter how much your outward circumstances may change.

In this regard, I'm reminded of how ephemeral and inadequate outward achievements, including wealth, can be. Consider a few recent reports, which might be summed up under the heading "How the High and Mighty Have Fallen" or perhaps "The Flaws of Fame and Fortune":

John Connally, former Texas governor and U.S. Treasury secretary, went into bankruptcy after a series of major business reverses. At one point he and a partner had assets of $300 million. But with the souring of the Texas economy and a string of bad luck in the mid-1980s, Connally and his partner found themselves owing $60 million and facing a score of lawsuits charging nonpayment of loans.

Saudi arms broker *Adnan Khashoggi,* once billed as the world's richest man, was unable to pay his bills in early 1987. The reason? He wasn't repaid an estimated $30 million he reportedly put up to underwrite U.S. arms delivered to Iran. As a result his duplex in the exclusive Olympic Tower in Manhattan was seized by court order to cover a $2.2 million debt he had failed to pay.

Nelson and W. Herbert Hunt of Texas, members of what was once regarded as the world's richest family, have become involved in litigation, trying to salvage part of their once-vast business empire. They overextended themselves in trying to corner the world's silver market and also made other questionable investments.

Ivan Boesky, once hailed as the premier investor in the arcane world of arbritrage and corporate takeovers, agreed to plead guilty to a felony, pay a $100 million fine, and quit Wall Street. His offense? He illegally used insider information to make profits of at least $50 million on takeover and corporate restructuring deals.

Clearly, there are many ways that the desire for material things can get out of hand or be frustrated by circumstances and personal business deficiencies.

When that happens there may be a tendency for your entire life to get out of control. You may become addicted to the desire for position, fame, or money, and thus experience not a resounding success, but a dismal failure.

How can you tell when you may be heading for danger? How can you know that you've lost a balanced sense of success and that you may be in the grip of a destructive addiction?

Many times, uncomfortable feelings about yourself or about a supposedly successful enterprise can tip you off. At a deep emotional level a number of indicators may signal that the drive to succeed is getting off track, becoming distorted, or leading to addiction. Think about, for instance, the messages that come across in the following sampling of headlines and journalistic reports:

"The Strange Agony of Success: Reaching the top—or making a million before 40—is unhinging many executives."[11] *The message:* You have to be emotionally and spiritually prepared to handle big success, or you may become too disturbed to enjoy the fruits of your labor.

"A Lot of Restaurants Now Serve Rudeness with the Rigatoni: Bad Manners Go Unchecked At Places Taking Success And Clientele for Granted."[12] *The message:* A lack of perspective and sense of humility about success may turn you into an arrogant achiever and a poor winner, flaws that will undercut your personal relationships and the possibility for future achievements.

"His Hart's Not in It Now: Donna ran with rich and famous. . . . Gary? He was small potatoes to Southern belle. . . . So Gary's quitting race for President.''[13] *The message:* A failure to observe basic moral values when you begin to succeed may cause you to fall down even more quickly than you rose to the top.

A story entitled "Feeling Poor on $600,000 a Year" explored how highly paid young investment bankers actually have trouble making ends meet as they feel compelled to keep up with the superrich.[14] Talk about a success addiction!

And then there was the confession by an accomplished film-making professional who once had a serious problem with alcohol and drugs. He reached the bottom when he went too far in indulging himself at a studio party and made a fool of himself in front of Dino De Laurentiis and other bigwigs. Although he managed to clean up his act and eliminate the substance abuse in his life, he found from that time on there was a limit on the assignments he could get.[15]

All this says that the dark, distorted side of ambition and achievement can undercut or completely destroy any chance for true success, and it can also seriously damage other facets of your life. A primary focus on the *rewards* of success rather than on the *essence* of success will inevitably upset not only the forward movement of your career, but also your relationships and the rest of your life.

On the other hand, no matter how addicted you've become, there's always hope of putting your life back in order and achieving a balance in your relationships, your career, and your inner life. One of the most dramatic events I've ever witnessed of how true success can be accomplished, even when all seems completely lost, began to play itself out before my eyes a few years ago in my pastoral work in Manhattan.

FROM DISMAL FAILURE TO TRUE SUCCESS

A thirty-eight-year-old woman whom I'll call Mary—a highly accomplished professional anthropologist—presented me with a very difficult assignment a few years ago. She told me that her doctors had just discovered she had cancer in four or five places in her body. She expected she had only a few months or, at the most, a year or so to live.

But her concern wasn't so much with her impending death as with her past life and her desire to set certain things right before she passed on. You see, about twenty years before that time, she had been married briefly, and during that marriage, she had given birth to a child. But she and her husband were far too young and immature for marriage at the time, so they decided to put the baby up for adoption.

Only a day or two after her little daughter was born, Mary relinquished the baby to the custody of the adoption authorities, and she and her husband got a divorce and went their separate ways. The only memento she kept of the tragic experience was a snapshot of the one-day-old infant.

As the years went by, Mary got some additional education, and she became interested in anthropology and ancient civilizations. So she threw her considerable energies and talents into researching how children lived in ancient civilizations. Eventually, she was recognized as a top leader in her field, and by practically any standard of career achievement, she would have been considered a success.

But deep inside Mary didn't feel completely successful. She knew that she had accomplished a great deal in her career. But there was that unresolved event twenty years ago, that little baby, who now must be almost a grown woman, living in some unknown spot, building her life completely apart from her real mother.

During the many years that had passed, Mary had never forgotten her child. Every year on the girl's birthday, she would find a church somewhere, enter the sanctuary, and say a little prayer. Then she'd write a letter to a state adoption agency and ask the officials there to put it into a folder, just in case the girl ever asked about her real mother.

When Mary discovered she had terminal cancer, she realized that very soon there would be no more opportunity for the prayers, thoughts, and occasional letters. If she ever hoped to re-establish any sort of relationship with her child, the time had arrived.

So she got in touch with me and said, "I have to find my little girl."

At first I tried to dissuade her because, as I said, "Twenty years is a long time. You don't know what may have happened to the girl in that time."

Mary was adamant, even though she was getting visibly weaker and it was becoming increasingly uncertain that a meeting could be arranged before her death. Despite my serious reservations about the final outcome, I agreed to conduct a search.

I faced some serious roadblocks from the very beginning. The original adoption organization Mary had used had gone out of business years before and another had emerged in its place. But I kept on the trail until I found a social worker who was willing to locate and contact the girl's adoptive parents, just to see if some sort of meeting could be arranged.

As it happened the adoptive parents and the girl were willing to meet with Mary. Then Mary got cold feet. On at least three separate occasions, she backed out of meetings we had set up with her daughter. Emotionally, she was unable to go through with it.

The thoughts running through her mind must have been excruciating: Will my daughter be angry with me? Is her hostility the last thing I'll have to remember when I leave this world? Will she blame me for abandoning her? How can she possibly understand what I was going through as a teenager?—How can she forgive me?

Finally, it became evident that Mary's last days were near. At the most she had only two or three weeks to live. She had left the hospital and was living at home, where she expected to spend her remaining time. She was in such bad shape that she needed oxygen regularly to supplement the little air she could take into her cancer-ravaged lungs.

During those final days, I got an urgent call from her. "I have to see my daughter," she told me when I arrived at her bedside.

"Are you sure about this?" I asked. "Your situation won't create the best atmosphere to establish a new relationship. Also, you're in no condition to deal right now with any difficult emotional confrontations. After all, you don't know a thing about this young woman. She may have some serious problems that you don't know anything about."

"No, this time I'm sure," she replied, in spite of the objections of her aunt, who had been helping to care for her during her illness. It took at least an hour of much crying and soul searching before we all agreed that the meeting should be arranged.

I can still remember vividly what, for me, was the turning point in my opinion about the matter. I told Mary, "You've got to be prepared for the possibility that this young woman is going to be furious with you. Do you really want to deal with such anger at this point in your life?"

"If all I receive from her is her anger, that will be enough for me," Mary replied firmly. "At the very least, I want that."

I immediately called the adoption organization, and the social worker there moved quickly to contact the adoptive parents. They were fine, sensitive, compassionate people. Within a few hours, they put together a photo album of the daughter's life that included pictures of the girl from the time she was adopted as a baby up to the present. As it turned out she was an outstanding student at one of the nation's leading universities.

At my suggestion Mary and her aunt responded with their own album, which described Mary's life and many accomplishments. She included a little essay on herself, along with some of her baby pictures.

Unfortunately, at this point Mary began to move in and out of consciousness. Sometimes, when I'd arrive at her home to visit her, she would be in a near-comatose state. At other times, though, she would be quite lucid, and in one of those clearer moments, she told me, "I only hope . . . I hope so much that I'll have a chance to see my daughter. These pictures"—and she pointed to the girl's album—"are so wonderful. I'd just like to be able to hold her hand."

But she was declining fast, and she seemed to spend more time unconscious than conscious. When I would spend an hour with her, she might be awake only five to ten minutes of that time.

Then, without warning, I found the daughter and her adoptive parents on my doorstep. "I want to see my mother," said the young woman, who looked much like a young, healthy version of Mary.

I explained how extreme the situation was and told them that Mary might have died already, but I'd certainly try to arrange something immediately. When I called the apartment, Mary's aunt answered and told me Mary was deep in a coma and wasn't expected to come out of it.

"It's only a matter of a few hours now," the aunt said. "Maybe even minutes. There's no way she can see anybody."

I put my hand over the phone and described the situation to the daughter, but she continued to insist on seeing Mary. The daughter said, "I just want to hold my mother's hand. I just want to see her."

Finally, the aunt agreed, and we all took a cab to Mary's apartment, hoping that we might at least get there before she died. When we entered the bedroom, Mary was, indeed, unconscious. With the idea of offering a kind of final benediction, I walked over to her, put my hand on her, and said a short prayer. To my utter amazement, her eyes opened, and she became completely lucid! She began to communicate perfectly, as though she wasn't even deathly ill!

As her eyes searched about the room, Mary immediately recognized her daughter, held out her arms, and enfolded the young woman in a lingering, maternal embrace. "I've always wanted to see you," Mary said. "I've thought about you constantly. But I was afraid I'd be rejected. It was only when I faced death that I found the courage to get in touch with you."

Mary took a ring off her finger—a ring that hardly would stay on because of the tremendous amount of weight she had lost—and placed it in her daughter's hand. Then she took a locket from around her neck and gave it to the girl. Inside was the single snapshot of the child who had been put up for adoption twenty years before.

As the daughter gazed at the picture and wiped the tears from her eyes, Mary slipped back into a coma. She died the next day with the knowledge that her life was more complete, more truly successful.

A few weeks later we had a memorial service at St. George's Church, attended by scholars from all over the country.

Shortly after the service, a university chair was named in honor of Mary. I invited her daughter for the occasion, and we both sat enthralled as we listened to the scholars praise Mary's achievements.

It was a privilege and joy for me to sit next to this beloved but missing daughter, who had always been an inspiration for Mary's outward accomplishments and who finally, at the last possible moment, had re-established a long-lost bond of love with her mother.

True success can't be defined as well in words as it can through the experiences of those who have achieved it.

CHAPTER SIX

HOW TO BE SURE YOUR JOB
IS NOT YOUR GOD

"Winning isn't everything. It's the only thing." These words, uttered by the late Vince Lombardi, former head coach of the Green Bay Packers, have come to symbolize the godlike quality of success in our culture. According to this creed, the only thing that matters is getting to the top, being the best, achieving the heights in your chosen field.

Even though many of us may secretly agree to one extent or another with Lombardi's words, in our heart of hearts, we have to take exception. As the humorist Roy Blount, Jr., has said, "It is worth reminding ourselves . . . that Lombardi's famous saying is crazy. The only thing that is everything is everything itself."[1]

To be fair to Lombardi, it's necessary to give equal time to one of his former linemen, Jerry Kramer, who played guard on several of the Packer championship teams. In an opinion article in the *New York Times*, Kramer offered this defense of his old coach's famous words:

> **Lombardi may have been a despot at times,**
> **but he was always an enlightened despot.**

In the first place, **Lombardi means winning fairly, squarely and decently—within the rules, the written ones and the unwritten. He would rather have lost than cheated.**

In the second, **Lombardi's definition of winning was not related directly to victory and defeat. He would rather have lost a well-played game than won a poorly played one. That may be a mild exaggeration, but this is not: He gave us more credit, and less grief, after a well-played defeat than after a poorly played victory.**[2]

Perhaps this explanation helps a little. But if you really believe that winning is everything, there's a good chance that winning, in the sense of achieving some sort of supersuccess, has assumed a godlike aura for you. When that happens you're well on your way to being entrapped by the American Success Cult and by the addiction to high achievement it fosters.

Take a close look at yourself. How can you prevent your job from becoming your god? The first step is to examine your attitude toward your work and the priority you assign to it.

In my personal relationships and counseling, I've encountered many people whose jobs have become their god. Their careers completely control every aspect of their lives, including personal time management, family interactions, and spiritual interests. If the demands of the job require it, they'll put work before family, friends, or religion. In effect they've fallen into the fallacy of affirming a kind of "career-faith," which has become the dominant force in their existence.

To help such people see the insidious forces at work in their lives, I've found it beneficial to think in terms of three career-faith fallacies, which highlight how much like a god their work has become. Take a look at each of these fallacies and see if they apply to you.

CAREER-FAITH FALLACY #1

Like a God, My Career Must Come
First Because It Can Provide Me
with Ultimate Meaning in Life.

In the film *Nothing in Common,* starring Tom Hanks and the late Jackie Gleason, Hanks plays a hotshot young advertising executive who finagles to secure a major airline account, which promises to make his career. Hanks uses all his charm, sexual and otherwise, and before long, he has the CEO and top staff of the airline in the palm of his hand.

But on the way up, Hanks runs into serious problems in his personal life. For one thing he can't seem to establish a long-term relationship with any woman. Also, he finds it impossible to get along with his cranky old father, played by Gleason. Gleason is not the most lovable person and certainly not the easiest to get along with. But you get the distinct impression as the movie moves along that Hanks could do more to improve his relationship with his dad and to get his own basic priorities in better order.

Finally, Hanks is presented with the ultimate choice for a serious career man. He finds himself under heavy pressure from the airline CEO to go out of town and give a crucial presentation for the airline account. Simultaneously, though, he's confronted with the need to stay home and be with his dad, who is all alone as he faces major surgery. The old man is paralyzed by fear, and Hanks knows from the doctors that his dad could die under the knife. But if Hanks stays at home, he has been told in no uncertain terms that he will lose the account.

He decides to stay to take care of his dad. As a result he loses the account, but his relationships with other people in his life immediately improve. Also, his boss at the ad agency turns out to be understanding. In the way that only a two-hour movie can do, we are presented with a telescoped, clear-cut choice involving priorities and the question of where to look for ultimate meaning in life.

As we've already seen in our earlier discussions of the concept of the calling, our obsession with career achievement in our culture has completely upset our fundamental priorities. Too often we expect an occupation to give us truth and meaning in life, when that kind of meaning can be provided only by more basic values and commitments, including the commitment to God Himself.

The late theologian-philosopher Paul Tillich understood this issue. Defining *religion* as a state of being grasped by "an ultimate concern about the meaning of one's life," he went on to describe *ultimate concern* as "taking something with ultimate seriousness, unconditional seriousness."[3] For Tillich this attitude represented religion in the broadest, most universal sense as opposed to what he called the "smaller concept" of religion, involving organized church denominations, clergy, and dogmas.

I certainly don't agree with all of Paul Tillich's

theology. In fact, I probably *disagree* with considerably more than I agree with. But I've found his broad definition of religion helpful because, on a daily basis, I see individuals giving their careers, success aspirations, and achievement levels a much higher priority than any other aspect of their lives. Their work becomes their religion, their object of ultimate concern, their god. And when this happens they inevitably end up feeling discontented, unconfident, and decidely *un*successful.

One man I know, Frank, had reached the top levels in a major American corporation. He wasn't yet the CEO, but he controlled the disposition of huge sums of money in buying and marketing goods and services for the general public. By almost any outward definition Frank was a resounding success. But sometimes all is not quite as it seems on the surface.

In a manner reminiscent of the bargain struck with Satan in Stephen Vincent Benet's story "The Devil and Daniel Webster," Frank had arrived at a kind of "deal" with himself early in his life. He had determined ever since he attended one of the nation's top business schools that he would devote his life to his career. Furthermore, he had resolved that nothing would stand in his way to achieve this end.

This strategy for the conduct of his life had crystallized just as he was finishing his graduate work in business. At a private farewell dinner, one of his professors had given him this rather disturbing advice: "Frank, you'll have to make an important decision early in your career. You'll have to make up your mind whether you'll put your career first or something else. If you put your career first, you'll succeed. If you don't, you won't. It's as simple as that. I've never known anyone who succeeded in a big way and still put family, friends, or anything else on a par with the job."

Frank thought long and hard about these words. It had been easy for him to become a high achiever because he had long ago gotten into the habit of trying to prove himself to both his peers and his parents. He had been a relatively poor athlete in school, and that deficiency had driven him to excel in other areas, such as his studies, intellectual activities like debate, and occasional entrepreneurial ventures. Also, both his parents constantly seemed to harp on his weaknesses rather than make him feel good about his strengths. He had never felt he really had their approval, but he kept trying to impress them through greater and greater achievements. So it was fairly easy for Frank to decide that his career meant more to him than anything else in the world. The money, power, and status that success in business would bring him might also provide that long-sought approval from other people.

Although he wasn't yet married, Frank rationalized that even with an unusually heavy emphasis on his career, he could probably still have a decent marriage and family life. He thought he might be able to play some regular golf and tennis as long as he could simultaneously promote his business interests by arranging the games with clients or colleagues at work. But he knew that if push came to shove, the career would have to prevail. Furthermore, he didn't see how a wife, children, or anything else could really satisfy him if somehow he fell short in his occupational aspirations.

After graduation, Frank didn't dwell consciously on this "bargain" he had made, but it became increasingly evident that his life was going to be controlled by the demands of his career. He married about a year after he entered the corporate world, and his wife, also a committed career person, seemed to fit into his lifestyle and value system quite well. Both decided they didn't want children right away—if they wanted them at all. The resulting lack of domestic entanglements made it easy for them to pursue their separate careers and still go out on social engagements together.

But then she was transferred to another city, and neither spouse was willing to compromise on where to live. Consequently they tried living apart during the week and commuting to see each other on weekends. But that didn't work because often both had to work or entertain clients on Saturdays and sometimes on Sundays. Soon their marriage was in serious trouble. Less than ten years out of business school, Frank found himself a divorced man who had become more compulsive than ever about his work and career.

Then the unthinkable happened. Frank began to lose interest in his job. This was a turn of events that no one would have predicted because Frank had always seemed to be a committed, chronic, unshakable hard-charger. "If there's one guy who will always have fire in his belly, it's Frank," observed one of his colleagues who had lost a promotion to Frank. "He'll always be able to generate enthusiasm for the job, no matter how hard he has to work or what's demanded of him."

Nevertheless, Frank's fire did finally go out. It was a gradual process that took place over the course of more than a year. First, he just couldn't get "up" for working those twelve- and fourteen-hour days. Then he started drinking an extra highball or two at night until he finally realized that alcohol was becoming a crutch to give him relief from the lack of fulfillment he was feeling on the job.

During this time Frank periodically became so depressed that a psychiatrist he had been seeing thought he should take prescription drugs to elevate his mood. The doctor actually worried at one point that he might be a suicide risk.

Life had lost much of its pleasure for Frank because he had lost zest for his work. He was proud of the business worlds he had conquered and the financial mountains he had climbed. But what challenges were left, except more of the same sort of worlds and mountains? Frank found that what he had chosen as his "ultimate concern" in life, his de facto religion, wasn't worth being such an overbearing top priority.

The full impact of his situation hit him when he began to date a woman who had two young children, a boy and a girl, with whom he became enthralled. He had never expected that kids could interest him so much, but he found himself wanting to help them with their schoolwork, athletics, and other youthful activities and challenges. He discovered that he harbored some very strong paternal instincts, which had been completely hidden as he had pursued the quest for ultimate meaning through his career.

With the combination of his burned-out condition at work and the positive tuggings he was feeling from the blossoming human relationships, Frank began to take steps to get his priorities in order. He eventually married the woman with the two children, and he assumed the role of stepfather with a commitment and an enthusiasm that had characterized his early years on the job—but with some major differences. He started to focus more on people than exclusively on promotions, profits, and multimillion-dollar projects.

What about Frank's top-level job? He still holds the same position, and he's still at his huge mahogany desk in that big corner office overlooking Manhattan. But even though many things seem the same from the outside, they turn out to be really quite different when you look a little closer.

With his personal priorities in better order, Frank's attitude toward his life has changed significantly. For one thing, he's no longer so compulsive about his work. Although he occasionally gets pulled into a late-night session when big deadlines are bearing down on him, he works much more reasonable hours than ever before and even insists that his subordinates do the same. He is also finding time to explore new interests, including true religion rather than the counterfeit variety of cultic success to which he had become addicted.

Has Frank's new approach to the meaning of life hurt his work? Not at all. His company is profitable, and he is considered one of the front runners for the position of CEO.

What we have here is a man who embarked on a quest for ultimate meaning in his work but failed miserably. At one point, with his destroyed marriage and devastated emotions, it seemed that he might lose, not only the sense of meaning he had derived from his career, but also any equilibrium in the other dimensions of his life.

Through a series of fortuitous circumstances, however, Frank got his priorities in better order, extricated himself from the clutches of the Success Cult, and escaped his addiction to distorted achievement. He is now on the way to true success and to the discovery of real meaning in his life.

CAREER-FAITH FALLACY #2

Like a God, My Career Will Last Forever.

God, by definition, is infinite and eternal; He has no beginning or end.

Your career, on the other hand, has a beginning and an end—and all too often the end comes much more quickly and abruptly than you hope or expect. Success and careers are not forever. You can't take them with you, and you may not be able to keep them intact when you're in the prime of life.

Let's consider a few cases in point.

Getting Fired. Sometimes you know it's coming. You may get signals from your boss or colleagues. Perhaps people start looking at you in a strange way, or they may just begin to avoid you. Somehow, even though you haven't been formally notified yet, the word is out that the ax is about to fall on you.

Len got these kinds of signals just after an announcement was made that his company was being taken over by a corporate raider. He was in the upper echelons of management and would be in a particularly vulnerable position when the acquisition of his firm was completed. It seemed quite likely that another top manager would move into his position, complete with the heady power that came from controlling billions of dollars' worth of transactions.

Len hoped that somehow he would be spared. "I'm valuable to them," he told his wife. "I expect they'll give me more consideration than some of the other executives."

It turned out to be nothing more than wishful thinking on Len's part. Len was apparently more valuable in his own eyes than in those of the new top executive. True to form in such situations, the ax did fall. When the takeover had been consummated, Len was told during a meeting with the new CEO that his services would no longer be required.

Len had been with his firm for his entire career, and he had trusted implicitly that somehow his company would always take care of him. As a result, he had failed to negotiate a "golden parachute"—a severance agreement that would have allowed him to walk away from his job a rich man. Certainly, he had accumulated a fair amount of money because of pension and profit-sharing arrangements, but his final compensation was nothing compared to what many other executives in his position were getting.

The impact on Len was devastating. At first he hoped to get another equally prestigious position immediately. He was only in his late thirties, and he expected that his track record would be quite attractive to other major companies.

Len did receive several generous offers, but in his mind, none equaled the job he had just lost. The salaries were all lower than the huge compensation he had been pulling in at his old company, and even more important was the lack of power he had enjoyed. Before, he had literally wielded control over billions of dollars. The new companies offered him authority over mere millions.

In Len's view he would be taking a step down to accept one of the new offers. With his need to achieve and operate at the top of the heap, he simply couldn't bring himself to do that. He continued to hold out for an even more attractive position, which his deeply held career-faith assured him was just around the corner. Len waited and waited, and the longer he waited, the more depressed he got. The job never materialized.

As we discussed his situation one day, it became evident to me that Len was one of those people who had expected his career to last forever. Of course, any intelligent person would acknowledge that nothing on this earth is going to last forever and certainly not any job. But too often we live as though our occupations will never end. We can't imagine not saying, "I'm the executive vice president of Acme Insurance," or "I'm a partner with the Jones and Jones law firm." Moreover, we develop no back-up systems—no spiritual life, significant noncareer goals, or deep personal relationships—that can cushion us if the job falls through.

Len is still trying to sort through his life, and I see some encouraging signs as he has been spending more time with his wife and children. His relationship with his family has improved significantly, and he's discovering for the first time what a great challenge it can be to nurture other people rather than his career.

In general I think it's helpful to approach the loss of a job as a former General Electric executive seems to have done when he was let go after his department was phased out. In an article appropriately entitled "Set Free," Richard B. Elsberry wrote, "After 25 or 30 years, work becomes an addiction like cigarette smoking, and one that is equally hard to break."[4]

While only in his early fifties, he was forced to break the addiction when G.E. terminated his employment. Now, as he receives reduced compensation from G.E. as part of his settlement, Elsberry is pursuing a long-desired occupation as a writer. To be sure he's not making as much money as he was before, but he has made the adjustment so well that he apparently can't imagine living any other way.

He commented,

I've finished 24 chapters of a book, and for the first time in my adult life I'm able, pretty much, to do all the things I've always wanted to do but never had the time for. Like taking my wife out for breakfast. Reading books I bought 10 years ago. Painting the house. Gardening. Fishing. Dreaming.

In breaking free of the corporate Success Cult Elsberry has discovered that it doesn't really matter that a job and career don't last forever. "I'm beginning to believe that being forced out of the corporate groove may be, next to my marriage, the best thing that ever happened to me," he concluded.

The Short-Term Career. In some cases a person may point his entire life toward the pursuit of one dazzling career that gives him a few starry moments of public acclaim. But such a career may have a limited life span. For a while it almost seems that the particular job is going to last forever, but inevitably it must come to a close. When that happens the individual involved must have some inner strength to fall back on, something that goes beyond the exhilarating "rush" accompanying dramatic, early, but short-lived success.

Dancers and professional athletes fall into this category. The *Wall Street Journal* ran an article about a member of Boston's ballet company, who at age twenty-seven was coming to the end of his career. "It's not the type of profession where you can pack up your desk and leave," the dancer said. "It's imprinted in your heart."[5]

Few ballet dancers continue with their art past the age of thirty, mainly because their bodies become worn out from the long, demanding daily hours of practice and rehearsals. Yet at the same time, few are prepared to embark on the next stage of their lives. This particular dancer planned to become a chiropractor, but it was evident he lacked the enthusiasm for his new field that he had demonstrated toward his dancing.

Dancers I've known who haven't made it as far as this man have sacrificed a normal childhood, often living away from home in faraway cities so that they could attend a recognized ballet school in an effort to perfect their skills. Everything in their lives has been directed toward the achievement of one goal, which in most cases would evaporate even before it had been fully achieved.

One young woman who came in for counseling lived

in New York for several years, beginning at age fourteen. She lived, ate, and breathed ballet until she was finally told, at about age eighteen, that she didn't have a chance to make a company. At this time she's still trying to piece her life back together after the disappointment; she's striving to find something other than a career that has more staying power in her life.

Serious professional athletes are in a similar situation and face just as many risks and devastating disappointments. Ted Plumb, for example, had wanted to be a football player almost all his life. He remembers telling his mother when he was in the fourth grade, "You have to promise me, Mom, that you'll let me play football!"

He went on to become a star split end for Baylor University and played in a couple of bowl games before he graduated in 1962. After he left college it was natural for Ted to take a shot at becoming a pro player since that's all he had ever really wanted to do. So he went to one of the pro teams in the Northeast to try out as a free agent.

But disaster struck. During a practice session Ted went for a pass and was tackled, hard. "I dove for the ball, and the defense guy drove me into the ground," he recalled. "Instead of bellying into the ground and sliding along on my stomach, or doing a somersault, I was driven into the ground like a javelin, headfirst."

At first Ted didn't realize how badly he was hurt, so he pulled himself up off the ground and tried to walk away. "But my hands were going numb, and I started crying and couldn't quit," he recalled. "I went to the trainer and said, 'I don't know what's the matter, but I can't quit crying. I don't know what's the matter with me.' I went to the hospital on a stretcher, with my head held in place by sandbags. My neck was broken, and some ribs were torn loose from my sternum."

Although the accident ended Ted's playing career, unlike many others in such a situation, he had a fall-back position. Certainly, he was temporarily devastated that his entire career had ended with that one tragic play. In fact, he became extremely depressed. But the Christian faith that had been nurtured in him since childhood began to take hold, and he sensed the presence of God becoming stronger and stronger in his life. "He gave me strength and showed me it wasn't my right to question why," Ted said. "And He helped me recall, 'Hey, remember you always wanted to eventually get out and help people in coaching? Well, here's your opportunity.'"

Ted did become a coach with the New York Giants and other teams. And just as important from his point of view, he participated actively in Christian work among pro athletes, helping others who were facing the end of an exciting but short-term career.

The Gold-Watch Syndrome. Even if you never get fired or never pursue a short-term career, you'll face retirement, unless you die before your working years have finished. At that time the satisfaction of achieving in the workplace will end. When you accept that gold watch or the equivalent on your last day on the job, the sense of identity you've derived from your career will be over.

Everyone who retires must, to one degree or another, wrestle with what I call the gold-watch syndrome—a complex of negative feelings and sometimes physical symptoms that accompany the loss of responsibility and status. For many retired executives, retirement becomes the ultimate example illustrating that money doesn't really matter all that much in life. In many cases retired top executives have plenty of money. They can do almost anything they want to do and travel wherever they want to go. But they lack all the other trappings that went along with their career success, and the vacuum in their lives can produce serious emotional and health crises.

One CEO at a Chicago advertising agency tried teaching and consulting just after he retired at age fifty-seven, and he was miserable for a year and a half! He didn't begin to find satisfaction and happiness again until he "realized that his professional achievements no longer mattered," one newspaper interviewer concluded after a session with him.

"Retirement forced me to reinvent myself," the executive said. He turned to one of his first loves—writing—and reported, "I've written one book [about retirement] and I'm struggling cheerfully to write another."

Finding some meaningful pursuit or outlet, other than the career, *before* retirement seems essential for those who want to avoid the gold-watch syndrome. But many of us are never quite willing to admit that our present careers are incapable of taking us onward and upward to some final height of personal fulfillment and satisfaction. It's often only at retirement that we are confronted with the stark reality of the third career-faith fallacy, the inability of a job to usher in the "abundant life" for us.

CAREER-FAITH FALLACY #3

Like a God, My Career Will Eventually Lead Me to the Abundant Life.

Jesus once said, "I have come that they may have life, and that they may have it more abundantly."[6] Yet ironically we often turn this statement around so that it says, "My career has come that I may have life, and that I may have it more abundantly." In other words, we expect our jobs to lead us to great happiness and fulfillment, and when that doesn't happen, the disappointment may be devastating or even deadly.

One woman, a prominent banker I knew for a number of years in New York, built her entire life around her need for independence, and her main vehicle for achieving this objective was a successful career. She was extremely well-educated, and she eventually reached the top in her field.

But she would allow nothing or no one to interfere with the priority she had given to her work and her independence. Even though she attended church services fairly regularly, she always kept her distance from any real experience with the faith. I learned from a series of discussions with her that she didn't like the idea of committing or submitting her life to anyone else, including God.

The need to remain in control and be her own person also kept her from getting married or becoming too closely involved with other people. To be sure, she had some friends, but she was careful not to get involved in "sticky" personal situations with them, such as supporting them during family or health crises. She had at least one opportunity to marry, but she decided not to because she didn't want to lose control over her life.

This woman's transition to retirement actually went rather smoothly. She had plenty of money from her investments and pension, and consequently, she found she could indulge her many outside interests, such as dining in top restaurants and traveling abroad. At first it really did seem that her career and the fruits she was enjoying in retirement had provided her with the abundant life.

But when she was in her eighties, she took a bad fall, broke her hip and leg in several places, and was confined to a wheelchair. She found that she had completely lost the independence she valued so highly. There was no way she could care for herself or take advantage of the money she had accumulated without having a nurse or other helper constantly by her side.

I had many discussions with her about the possibility of entering fine retirement home facilities where she could live well and enjoy expert care, but she rejected any such suggestions. "I'd rather die than live out my life that way," she said.

Some of her relatives who lived in another part of the city came up with what I believed was a thoughtful and generous offer. They said they would arrange for her to move in next to them, and they also volunteered to help care for her and manage her affairs. It seemed that we had found a solution to this woman's problem, and she appeared amenable to the idea.

But one week before she was supposed to make a final decision about the move, this elderly lady chose another way. Making a supreme effort, she managed to pull herself out of her wheelchair, climb up to a window, and jump to her death from her sixth-floor apartment.

There's no guarantee that any career or retirement plan will produce the abundant life for anyone. In fact, the opposite seems true. In every case I've encountered there has apparently been an implicit kind of guarantee that the career, by itself, *won't* lead to the abundant life. It's essential for each of us, as early as possible, to recognize that there are limits to the satisfaction and happiness our work can provide.

In this regard I'm reminded of a young certified public accountant (CPA), a committed Christian whom I'll call Ron, who worked in one of the nation's largest accounting firms. From the outset he made it clear to his superiors that he had important outside interests, including his family and his church work. He refused to work late hours because that took him away from his wife and children. He also insisted on keeping some evenings and all Sundays open so that he could attend worship services and do charitable work, including working with the destitute in a major urban area.

This young man's senior partner, whom I knew on a social basis, once confided to me, "You know, Ron has a lot of ability, but I'm afraid he's just not tough enough to make it in the New York professional world. He just isn't willing to commit himself and put in the hours."

But Ron *was* committed—to different values from those the senior CPA recognized. As it happened Ron eventually left the firm and found a job with a lower-pressured company that allowed him more time to pursue his charitable interests.

At this point, of course, Ron is not as old as the female banker was who committed suicide, so it's not clear how he'll experience the abundant life in his later years. But I'm convinced that so long as he stays on his present track with the spiritual values he has already affirmed so deeply, he *will* experience the real abundant life in some form.

This young accountant and others like him have impressed me with how important it is to recognize early on that winning and success aren't everything. Only God is. A job can never be an adequate substitute for God. Only He—and the values and principles He represents—can provide the ultimate, lasting sense of meaning and the genuine abundant life that we all, down deep, hunger and long for.

THE SECRET POWER OF
SHARED SUCCESS

Popular caricatures portray the successful person as an individual who is self-possessed, self-confident and, more often than not, self-centered. You've heard the critical litany:

"He may be successful, but he's had to step on a lot of people to get there."

"She may have achieved a lot in life, but she's not a very nice person."

"Those two may be a supercareer couple, but they certainly don't lift a finger to help people less fortunate than themselves."

Such statements aptly describe many people I know, especially self-centered younger people who are still climbing the ladder toward the top in their fields. But they aren't completely successful. They haven't reached the point where they've learned to enjoy and take advantage of their achievements to the fullest. They lack a special source of power in their lives, one that can enhance their personal enjoyment and satisfaction and significantly improve the lives of other people. They've fallen short of the many exciting possibilities that accompany *true* success.

With true success, which combines inner satisfaction and peace with outward accomplishments, there will always be a beneficial "fall-out effect"—a helpful impact on others that reaches beyond isolated individual achievement. To put this another way, it's necessary for the individual to step outside himself and lend a helping hand to others if he hopes to enjoy the full benefits of his accomplishments. This special power that becomes his when he begins to share success is a power that can bring a multitude of emotional and material benefits back to the already successful person who has chosen to share his blessings; greatly improve the physical and emotional circumstances of other people; and perpetuate and broaden the impact of a person's success over a wide geographical area and for many years into the future.

But what exactly is involved in "sharing" success with others? Is it just a matter of devoting a few hours a week to helping others or donating a few thousand dollars a year to charity? Or is something more required?

As we try to answer these questions, let's first consider some average and some not-so-average standards of sharing by achievement-oriented people.

WHAT ARE OUR SOCIETY'S STANDARDS OF SHARING SUCCESS?

The higher you move in your chosen field, the more you'll probably be expected to give some extra money and time to charity. You may be asked to serve on the board of a nonprofit community organization or as honorary chairperson of some philanthropic fund-raising cause. Or you may feel a nagging responsibility to respond in other ways to the needs of those in your local community who are less fortunate than you.

According to a Gallup report on top achievers,[1] the average successful person devotes 3.1 hours a week to volunteer activities. Those with incomes of $200,000 a year or more put in an average 4.7 hours a week sharing their success through such noncareer work. Other studies have revealed that many successful people contribute an average of about 3 percent of their incomes to charities, about $3,000 for those with annual earnings of $100,000.

Such time and monetary commitments may require some extra effort and financial planning, and they may also present some scheduling problems for extremely busy executives. But on the whole this kind of sharing with others seems manageable for most people.

Perhaps the ultimate example of the successful person who contributes a substantial (but apparently not personally painful) amount to others is thirty-eight-year-old Sir Muda Hassanal Bolkiah, the sultan of Brunei, a small kingdom on the north coast of Borneo. As part of his altruistic efforts, the sultan has avoided levying a personal income tax on his two hundred thousand subjects, whose yearly per capita income is reported to be $22,000. Most of his citizens seem to live in simple little seaside homes, though there are many TV antennas, air conditioners, and outboard motorboats in evidence. So at least by Third World standards, the citizens of Brunei appear to be doing all right as beneficiaries of the sultan's largesse.

On the other hand, the sultan is doing pretty well himself. Billed as the world's richest man by the 1984 *Guinness Book of Records* and the second-richest billionaire in a 1987 *Forbes* magazine report, he lives in a 1,788-room palace, which reportedly cost $300 million to build. He owns 350 polo ponies, several Boeing jets, a caravan of more than 100 cars, and real estate and other investments around the world worth billions. Clearly, then, even though the sultan may have an altruistic streak, he's not subjecting himself to any serious sacrifices. His gifts to others certainly don't prevent him from living in the luxurious style to which he has become accustomed.[2]

But let's be fair. It's easy to single out the sultan in this way because he's so visible. A much less generous approach to sharing success characterizes many of the high achievers in our society. Often their charitable involvements, if they have any at all, are nothing more than gestures. Most modern-day achievers don't appear to be making any radical sacrifices in giving their time or money to others.

Is this really what the secret of shared success is all about? No, it's not. At the beginning of the upward climb toward big achievement, it may be all right to go slowly and take on only those volunteer commitments that, at the most, may be slightly bothersome in light of your pressing time commitments. Or you may initially give of your financial resources in relatively small amounts. You may, in effect, just shell out a little extra pocket change, which you'd normally prefer to spend on something else.

But the experience of sharing that I'm talking about can't stop here, at least not if you hope to enjoy the full effect of the giving of yourself to others. On the contrary, considerably more is required. The basic standard of shared success—the standard that helps open the door to real inner power and true success—is nothing less than what in an earlier day might have been called servanthood.

THE POWER OF THE SUCCESSFUL SERVANT

When you think about success and power in our culture, probably the *last* thing that comes to mind is being a servant. By definition, a servant in our society cannot be successful. Sometimes, in certain rags-to-riches scenarios, a person may begin as a servant, but he invariably works his way up, out of that lowly state, to the top of the ladder where he can hire and direct others who remain servants. In any case, the truly successful person doesn't end up as a servant, or at least, this is the attitude many of us have toward that humble state.

I'd like to suggest a somewhat different approach, one I must hasten to say isn't original with me. Jesus expressed it quite well when He said, "Whoever desires to become great among you shall be your servant."[3] Is it really possible to be a *real* success and a servant at the same time? Aren't the two roles incompatible?

Many people attempt to achieve complete success without also incorporating a radical commitment to service in their lives. I think that when this happens it's almost inevitable that success will become distorted and lead to that cultic type of addiction we've already explored. So I always advise those people who are ascending the ladder of worldly success to be constantly vigilant about their commitment to servanthood.

I get my cue here from St. Basil, the great fourth-century leader of the movement toward communal asceticism and monasticism. He was always ready to promote the ideals of servanthood, even among those who seemed already committed to spiritual success and greatness.

As one story goes, when he was told about the great wonders and miracles that St. Antony, a Christian hermit living in the desert, was performing, Basil listened quietly until his awed informant had finished. Then he asked quietly, "Whose feet does he wash?"

That's a question I regularly ask myself, and one I would urge you to put to yourself periodically: *Whose feet do I wash?*

The act of washing feet has, since ancient times, been associated with humble service. Perhaps the most memorable example of this practice occurred in the Upper Room during the Last Supper. There, Jesus laid aside His outer clothing, wrapped a towel around Himself, poured water into a basin, and began to wash His disciples' feet. Peter, realizing what a humble occupation this was, protested, "You shall never wash my feet!" But Jesus answered, "If I do not wash you, you have no part with Me."[4]

At that time Jesus was at the very height of His messianic mission, on the verge of the crucifixion and the resurrection. Yet His ultimate success, in the sense of

fulfilling His main mission in life, coincided with ultimate servanthood.

On occasion I've mentioned to various high
achievers the rather unusual idea that there should be
a link between great success and servanthood. And immediately, I've been met with a multitude of objections:

"You're living in a dream world, Tom! You can't
reach the top and still carry along this biblical bag-
gage!"

"Such servanthood may have been fine for Jesus
and the hermits and the monks through the ages. But
that just won't work in our society."

"That's not a very efficient concept, is it, Tom? I
mean, it doesn't really make sense for a top executive
to waste a lot of time replaying the lowly, subordinate
roles he had as a younger person. A successful person
can do a lot more good by *hiring* a servant rather than
becoming one!"

"This servanthood idea won't work because it goes
against basic human needs and concepts of fairness.
After all, nobody who has worked hard all his life, who
has scratched and fought to get to the top, should be
expected to give that up and start waiting on other
people!"

I find these objections are voiced most often by
those who have not yet reached full success. On the
other hand, for those who have been recognized as
the most successful in our culture, the acceptance of
the power of servanthood is much more widespread.
For example, in a Gallup survey of individuals listed
in Marquis's *Who's Who*, more than half—51
percent—of the top achievers said that they regarded

"caring about other people" as an extremely important personal trait that had contributed to their success.

In practical terms, how do you go about caring for
other people? And how do you find a reasonable balance between being a servant and being a success?

HOW SHOULD YOU SHARE
YOUR SUCCESS?

I've found at least three major principles that, if followed, will enable you to share your success so as to
generate tremendous power in your life.

Principle #1: You Must Make Great
Servanthood One of the Major Goals
in Your Life.

Just as you set goals to achieve worldly success, you
should also strive to expand and deepen your service
commitments and activities. In my opinion your service should begin with your family, friends, and loved
ones who are closest to you, but your expressions of
servanthood should also reach out to the needy in
your local community and beyond.

I'm reminded of one father, a very successful executive, who knew he was devoting plenty of time to his
work and to various personal projects and activities.
However, he sensed he was not giving enough time to
his wife and especially to their young son.

As he tried to evaluate a typical week in his life, he
found he was having trouble remembering how much
quality time he actually spent with his family. To him

"quality time" meant those periods that involved talking directly, in edifying ways, with his wife and child or otherwise interacting with them.

To ascertain more precisely how much of this quality time he was giving to his wife and son, he kept track of what he did with his waking hours over the course of one week, and he was shocked by what he discovered. He devoted only about a half-hour a day to meaningful personal interactions with his wife and a mere ten to fifteen minutes a day with his son.

What was he doing instead of being with his family? Although he often got home in time for the evening meal, on most days he went directly from the dinner table to his newspaper or to the TV set, and that was the last his family heard from him. One or two evenings a week he would play tennis for a couple of hours with a friend.

Clearly, he needed to make some changes. So to monitor his time and be sure his family didn't get squeezed out by work commitments or other activities, he decided to keep a time log each day of the quality time he spent with his wife and son. Before long, he got up to an hour and fifteen minutes with his wife and an hour with his son. He readily acknowledges today that his new-found family time will quickly disappear if he stops setting definite goals or keeping strict records of how he spends his nonworking hours.

Principle #2: You Should Think in Terms of Sacrificial Giving of Your Time and Money.

It may be helpful to set out on the road to servanthood by doing a little for others or by giving away a little of your money. But if you hope to experience the full benefits, you can't stop with just a little time, effort, or giving. In fact, it may be necessary to give of your time and money to the point that it begins to hurt, to the point that you have to start choosing between doing things for yourself or doing things for others.

Consider what it means to give sacrificially from your financial resources. It won't do just to give from the funds you really don't need. You may need to give to the point that you have to choose not to buy certain things for yourself.

As you may know, the Bible frequently refers to the tithe, or one-tenth of one's income, as the basic standard for material giving. I believe that one reason the tithe has been chosen is that this percentage of personal income stretches the commitment of most people. It's a tough standard to maintain.

One very successful Christian accountant, who regularly earned more than $100,000 annually and also built up equity as a partner in a firm, had made a decision with his wife at the beginning of his career to give a *minimum* of a tithe. In the early years it was sometimes hard for the couple to make ends meet and still live up to that commitment.

Even at this man's present income level, he sometimes finds himself financially pinched after paying for his children's schooling, his living expenses, and contributions of as much as 20 to 25 percent of his income. Recently he and his family decided to take a relatively low-budget vacation near their home rather than go on a planned trip to the Far West. The reason?

After they made a large contribution to a ministry to the poor, they simply didn't have the money available for a more luxurious holiday.

In discussing his finances and investments with his financial adviser, this accountant was told, "You really could do a lot better if you didn't give so much money away! Think of the extra trips you could take with your family or the extra things you could buy!"

At times, the idea of cutting back on his giving has been tempting. But as he said to me, "I wouldn't trade the last inexpensive vacation we took for anything. Somehow, we seemed closer as a family on that trip—in part because everyone understood that we were making a sacrifice in order to give away additional money to those who are less fortunate than we are."

By any outward, material standard, this accountant is successful. Moreover, I don't think he has become any less successful because he has elected to divert money he might have spent on himself to those who are more needy. In his case I'd say that his sacrificial giving has made him even *more* successful!

The same approach applies to your time. When you give of your time, it may be helpful to think in terms of devoting enough hours to the welfare of others so that you feel pushed by your commitment. I'm not saying, of course, that you should overdo your commitment to the point that you get burned out or your other important relationships suffer. However, successful servant-hood, like a successful career, becomes truly meaningful and reflects significant involvement only after you really throw yourself into helping a needy individual or working on a particular service project.

Principle #3: It's Necessary to Get Involved in Person-to-Person Service.

You may be called upon to use your talents in helping various service organizations, which is a worthy and commendable way to spend part of the time you've allotted for service. But it won't do to devote *all* your time to working on committees or to limit your charitable work to giving away your money or in other ways to deal with needy people at a distance. Some substantial part of your service to others must be devoted to individual, personal involvement with those who need help. Otherwise you're likely to find that you're running, leading, and achieving in your service work on the same terms that you're achieving with your regular job.

Donald V. Seibert, former chairman and chief executive officer of the J.C. Penney Company, seems to have understood this principle well. While he was at Penney, Seibert served as national chairman of the United Way campaign and also on a number of nonprofit committees and boards. Yet he also made time for getting involved with individuals.

For one thing, he spent a considerable amount of time meeting and working with young people, including students who were trying to make important decisions about their careers. Many of his lunch hours were set aside for these counseling sessions.

At his church he could have assumed the role of a respected but distant elder "spiritual statesman." Instead, at one point he chose to work as an aide in the nursery department so that the parents of the youngsters could attend services.

"No matter how little you think you know or have to

offer, there are many who can benefit from your experience," Seibert says.

> I believe each of us, at various levels of achievement in business, has a responsibility to share what he knows with those on lower levels. Taking the initiative to help those below you—including students who haven't even entered the working world—will strengthen the entire business system.[5]

True servanthood depends heavily on such person-to-person interaction and help. Without in-depth personal involvement with others, it's likely your attempts to become a real servant will falter and finally fail.

Some or all of these principles may seem totally unrealistic and completely unworkable in real-life situations. But I've *seen* them work in individual lives. Furthermore, I know that this sort of radical sharing of success is absolutely necessary for anyone who hopes to keep ambition and the drive toward achievement in proper perspective.

As you get more deeply involved in serving other people, you'll experience some of the power that shared success can bring. For one thing you'll very likely find that *you* are reaping most of the benefits! Donald Seibert puts it this way:

> I've known many people who have spent vast amounts of time or money on a particular person or project without any expectation of getting

**anything in return. They gave out of the good-
ness of their hearts, and weren't even looking for
a thank-you. Yet weeks, months, or even years
later the person or organization they helped
crossed their path again and returned the original gifts they had given many times over. In
a number of cases, that unexpected return on
investment came from a staff person who
strengthened the entire organization and played
a key role in a later promotion of the executive
who had originally provided the help.**[6]

There are many ways that sharing your success can
inject additional power into your career and your personal life. There are potential outward benefits, which
will accrue to you as people respond positively when
they see how committed you are to the welfare of
others. There are also inner benefits, such as the feeling of doing some good for another person or of having made life a little more bearable for the needy.

In addition, your service will improve the entire
community and organizations of which you are a part.
By contributing your "two cents" to improve the circumstances of a particular person or situation, you'll
enhance the well-being and efficiency of the group as
a whole. And you'll transform your surroundings into
a more pleasant and helpful environment for future
generations.

Finally, you'll find that serving others will help you
keep your basic values, including your approach to
success, in order. It's very difficult, if not impossible,
to lose perspective on yourself and your achievements
when you're deeply involved in helping those less for-

tunate than you. One of the best insurance policies against being entrapped by the Success Cult and becoming addicted to the distorted values of certain types of achievement is to learn some of the secrets of sharing your success.

CHAPTER EIGHT

THE FEMALE MISTAKE

A number of years ago, when I was chairman of a special children's program, I had the opportunity to serve on the board with the great anthropologist Margaret Mead. In fact, she followed me as chairperson of the group.

Although Dr. Mead achieved great things in her field, she engaged in many difficult personal struggles during her life, especially in her relationships with men. Until the very end, when she died at age seventy-six in 1978, she had unresolved feelings about marriage, her sexuality, and her intimate personal interactions.

Many of the deep questions she harbored about human relationships resulted from her broad research into a variety of divergent societies as well as from her sometimes untraditional personal moral views and lifestyle. In her heart of hearts, though, she always seemed to affirm the importance of traditional marriage, family life, and the distinct roles of men and women in our society. Yet she feared that those with special natural gifts and strengths were failing to use their assets, to the detriment of our culture as a whole.

She once told me, "One of the biggest problems in this country is that grandparents have abdicated their responsibilities. The key to any successful society is active grandparents because they help children understand their parents and parents cope with their children. Grandparents can stabilize a society as they promote a general atmosphere of communication and as they lessen the explosive nature of family life."

By the same token, Margaret Mead felt that women were in many ways abdicating their special voice and insights. Instead of being happy as women and trading on their unique female strengths, too often they were modeling themselves after men. And that, in Dr. Mead's view, was a major mistake.

She confided to me that she wasn't excited about the ordination of women in the Episcopal church, which occurred in 1976. Of course, her objection wasn't that she wanted to hold women back in inferior, less powerful positions. On the contrary, she wanted them to exercise a more legitimate and beneficial kind of power than she perceived the male clergy had done. Yet as she saw it, many women were just buying into the same self-centered ambition and upward ecclesiastical movement that had always characterized the male clerics.

"I really can't get very interested in this women's ordination business," she told me. "Most of the male priests and bishops I know are involved in wielding the wrong kind of power. And the women I know are falling right into the same trap. They're just assuming the same corrupt attitudes and values the men have."

Margaret had hoped that women priests could develop a different, improved approach to the use of power. But in her view the women seemed to be relying on the same power plays, blind ambition, and narrow, highly secular views of success and achievement that had usually characterized the men. So as Margaret watched the general trends in the church, she became disillusioned and began to wonder if it was worth it for women to become ordained at all.

What Margaret Mead saw in the female clergy reflects the crux of the Female Mistake, both inside and outside the church: Working women have failed to perceive the deficiencies in the traditional male approach to success, and they have neglected to find more valid standards and models to follow.

A tremendous surge of women into the working world has occurred during the last two decades so that in 1987 women comprised 45 percent of the work force.[1] There are many reasons for this development, including the increasing influence of the feminist movement; the growing desire of bright, capable women to succeed in business and the professions, and the prevalent economic necessity for both spouses in many families to bring home paychecks.

Unfortunately, however, instead of using her new opportunities to change things for the better, the typical career woman usually marches to the drumbeats that have guided men throughout our history. Without thinking, she falls automatically in line behind her male counterparts and leaders. Most working women fail to ask, Is there something distinctive that I can do to make my drive toward success a more human and satisfying experience?

It's important to be both fair and realistic in making such observations. The power structures in our society are very seductive and forceful in moving women as well as men toward an addiction to the distorted contemporary approach to success. The prospects of great prestige, power, and money can work their wiles as effectively on women as on men, with the result that the need to achieve, attain, and acquire get increasingly out of hand.

One indication of the power of the Success Cult emerged in a survey of four thousand career women by *Working Woman* magazine in 1985.[2] In that study nearly two-thirds of the total women surveyed said they would need an annual salary of $100,000 to feel rich, but this was just the beginning. The amount required for that "rich feeling" increased as the salaries of the women increased. For example, 40 percent of those earning $60,000 or more said they couldn't feel rich with a mere $100,000; they needed $500,000!

By almost every standard, many women who have entered the work force in the last few years have slipped into the Success Cult and become addicted to the values of success just like their male colleagues. A self-centered, achievement-obsessed, put-business-first attitude has gripped bright, upwardly mobile women much as it has gripped many men.

This Female Mistake greatly disturbs me. In my encounters with success-oriented women, I've become acutely aware that established, committed career men are not the best role models for younger men, women, children, or anyone else.

WHY MEN ARE NOT THE BEST MODELS

There are a number of reasons why I believe the average career man is a terrible model for the career woman. Consider a few that have become apparent to me in recent years.

1. Most career men are entrapped to some degree by the American Success Cult. No rational person really wants to look to this webwork of distorted values and relationships as a compelling standard.

2. Many men have become so addicted to greater and more impressive achievements that their careers have often taken first place in their lives, above their families, God, and everything else.

3. Men—even those with working spouses—have traditionally relinquished the role of primary caretaker of the children to their wives. But I've found that most working women, when they really think about it, don't want to push aside the joys of child rearing as men have.

4. Many men who are caught up in the drive to succeed fail to develop a decent husband wife bond. Because of the pressures on their time and their preoccupations with work, they neglect their wives. They may prefer to deal with their spouses almost as business colleagues and approach family problems on a detached, cerebral basis rather than on the "messier" but often more healing level of feelings.

These features certainly don't provide a very attractive model for women to emulate. Yet many career women, in their near-frenzied need to prove themselves in a "man's world," may fall into the trap of

modeling themselves after these and other male flaws
and failings—with quite unhappy results. To get some
idea of the dangers, let's take a look at the difficulties
and disappointments of some actual women who have
wrestled with the Female Mistake.

The Failure of Family Life

There's a tremendous temptation for bright, career-
oriented women to give their jobs a priority over many
of the more traditional joys and responsibilities of
family life. One factor is the extra money that's often
involved in delaying childbirth. Women who wait to
have their first child until after they are twenty-seven
years old can make 36 percent more in salary than
those who have their first child before age twenty-two.
This finding comes from an analysis by Harvard's
David Bloom of data from the U.S. Bureau of the Cen-
sus.[3]

In practice, however, a delay in childbearing may
also lead to no children at all. According to a 1982
Korn-Ferry International study of three hundred executive women, only 39 percent of the female achievers
said they were mothers. As a *Business Week* reviewer
noted in citing this study, "If motherhood is used as a
measure, women who achieve business or professional success are failures."[4]

A very human illustration of this point came home
to me as I considered the frustrations faced by one
young career woman who came to me for help. Both
she and her husband were successful professionals,
he in advertising and she in television, and they com-
muted to work each day in a limousine. They belonged

to the best health and social clubs, ate out almost every night at the best restaurants, spent weekends at their $1.5 million country estate, and vacationed in the world's most exclusive resorts.

But despite all these outward signs of success, this woman was profoundly unhappy. Already in her late thirties, she sensed strongly that her "biological time clock was ticking," as she said. She knew that time was running out if she hoped to have any children, and the lack of a child was clearly the factor producing deep sadness in her life.

As we talked, it became obvious to both of us that the time had arrived for her and her husband to make a major decision about children. If they didn't decide soon, the decision would be made for them by her advancing age. But from her viewpoint the decision was almost too difficult and painful to confront. In the first place, if she decided not to have a child, she worried that she would regret the lack of offspring for the rest of her life. On the other hand, if she decided she would try to get pregnant, that move would trigger a whole series of other decisions and events that she suspected would threaten her hard-won achievements at work.

So, what was this woman to do? She and her husband decided to go ahead and have a child, and within about a year, she became pregnant. She has had the baby—a girl now about a month old—and the new mother is *still* trying to decide how she will juggle a career and the responsibilities of family life. But the presence of her new daughter has caused her to reevaluate the priorities she had given to her career.

Among other things, she says she may cut back on her work responsibilities for a while, at least until she can get her new family situation on an even keel.

This woman expects to return to the career world, and I expect that when she does, she'll have a more balanced, effective, and happier approach to success. I already see a significant improvement in her level of satisfaction with life.

Anthropologist Patricia A. McBroom, in *The Third Sex: The New Professional Woman* (New York: William Morrow, 1986), has reported similar responses by executive mothers in her study of the feelings and attitudes of forty-four top-level corporate women. She has found that fifteen of the female executives had children, and those fifteen mothers were the happiest and most successful of the entire group studied.

But make no mistake about the wrenching decisions that may be required if you plan to try to have a successful career *and* a full family life. In a 1986 survey by Heidrick and Struggles, Inc., female executives were asked which areas of their personal lives had been most affected by their careers. Their responses went like this:

- 30 percent said their decision to have children.
- 17 percent said the success of their marriages.
- 15 percent said their choice to marry at all.
- 13 percent said their effectiveness as parents.

Success-oriented women, perhaps even more than men, face great challenges in maintaining a satisfying, rewarding family life. As we've seen, issues relating to parenthood seem to create the most problems. But questions about love and marriage come in a close second. So let's focus more on the special difficulties that may plague the successful woman's love life.

The Loss of a Love Life

As competent, highly motivated women get deeply involved in moving ahead at top speed on a fast track in their careers, many neglect their relationships with the opposite sex. To be sure most of these upwardly mobile women date, and at one time or another, they may even get serious about a man. But often they make an unspoken assumption, *There's still time for me. I don't have to panic about marriage. Right now, my career comes first. Later, I'll settle down with a man.*

You've heard these assumptions expressed, and you may have even bought them yourself at some point. There's a time and place for everything, including a successful career and a successful marriage. You just have to put first things first. Give yourself plenty of time to achieve your career goals, and then you can get married and have a family.

In the perfect world that we create as we plan for our futures, we may *hope* that our lives will proceed in such a neat, orderly sequence, but the real world isn't perfect. As far as love is concerned, our personal worlds can get very unpredictable and unmanageable indeed.

The great actress and dancer Ginger Rogers seems to have discovered this fact after her impressive film achievements were already behind her and she had finally settled back to reflect on her life. In an interview with Dotson Rader, Rogers said, "I don't get physically lonely. Not yet. I don't mind being alone."[5]

Then she almost seemed to contradict herself when
she confided,

> **Sometimes it's not easy. It'd be fun to have a
> chum around, but it's very hard to have a chum
> unless you're married to him, and I don't believe
> in today's concept of living with someone un-
> married.**
>
> **It's either marriage or be alone. There was a
> time, five or six years ago, when I was looking
> around for someone. I'd see a man and think,
> "My, isn't he good-looking; maybe he has a good
> sense of humor." Or, "This one seems so
> bright." But I decided what I was doing was
> wrong: Why be unhappy over what isn't possible
> without marriage? When two people love each
> other, they don't look at each other. They look in
> the *same direction*. It's very hard to find some-
> one who looks in the same direction.**

Her observations sum up quite well a major source
of conflict between success and marriage. For a marriage between two equally committed career-oriented
people to work, each partner must understand and respect the other's inner drive to achieve. They must be
able to look *together* at their career goals as well as at
other aspects of their relationship. Yet somehow, at
the same time, each must see the way to give priority
to their marriage, not to their careers. That is a tall
order!

Apparently, Ginger Rogers was never able to find
the right combination of a career and a satisfying love
life. "I don't want to live without love," she said.

I love to be loved, of course. I love people to show their affection to me. I'll never be above that.

Somehow, it's just gone past me—not love, but all that goes with it. I miss not having a family, but maybe I should be glad, because so many children get involved in drugs or go to jail or kill themselves. . . . So maybe it's good I didn't have children.

I heard similar expressions of regret from a thirty-five-year-old female doctor who had modeled herself after her highly successful father, who was a prominent Chicago attorney. Unlike Ginger Rogers, this woman, because of her relatively young age, was in a stronger position to reclaim the love she felt her life-long emphasis on career had caused her to miss.

This physician had devoted her early adult years to excelling at her career, and she had moved up to a position of great prominence in her specialty. But always, it seemed, she worked those long, hard hours in an effort to match the example her father had set for her. In a sense the father had looked upon this woman, the older of two daughters, as the son he had always wanted but never had. The hopes and aspirations he might have placed upon a boy had instead found their way to the shoulders of his elder daughter.

Although she loved her father dearly, she could never remember a time when he wasn't focused in some way on work. The stories he told at the dinner table, the conversation during family vacations, and the personal advice he gave her about life always centered somehow on his career—and on the successful career he wanted her to have.

When this young woman entered medicine, she worked with an exclusive emphasis on achieving top honors and accolades in her field. Her human relationships focused almost entirely on people who could help her in her career. Her mind consistently wandered to other subjects when anyone began to discuss personal concerns not related to her work. The possibility of finding a spouse or beginning a family didn't even enter the picture—at least not until she reached her midthirties and realized that her options to get married and have children were fast being closed down.

Fortunately for her, when this realization hit her, she already had a couple of ardent, eligible suitors, even though she hadn't paid much attention to them before that point. After we talked and she got a better perspective on her situation, she became more interested.

Finally, she accepted a proposal of marriage from one of these men, and during their engagement she worked hard at leaving behind the career-obsessed legacy she had inherited from her father. She made a special effort to become sensitive to the needs and feelings of her fiance. She also learned to listen closely to him as well as to others, and she found that she was gradually becoming less preoccupied with her work and more interested in the lives of other people.

I'm not suggesting that it's essential for everyone to get married. Nor am I saying that you can't possibly have a happy, satisfying life unless you are married. What I *am* saying is that there are people and values in this world more important than your career. Unless you recognize this fact and live as though it's true, you may well find yourself on a road that could lead to a loss of love in your life.

The Threat to Health

The Female Mistake, which characterizes women who have modeled their lives after distorted male success values, may also pose a serious threat to health and even to life. Too often an excessive or exclusive emphasis on achievement or perfection may result in one or more of a wide variety of emotional and physical difficulties, including debilitating anxiety, depression, eating disorders, and drug or alcohol abuse.

These health problems may arise because of the achiever's need to exercise complete control over some aspect of her life. Or they may appear because the person needs some way to release the pent-up pressures and stresses that constantly bear down upon her. Or there may be a variety of other specific causes. Whatever the reason for the problem, serious danger may be just around the corner unless something is done to relieve the compulsive need to achieve and succeed.

Many high-achieving women have wrestled with eating disorders, such as anorexia nervosa and bulimia. Successful young actress, Ally Sheedy, has had this problem. Having starred in movies like *WarGames*, *The Breakfast Club*, and *St. Elmo's Fire*, Sheedy has excelled in a variety of fields in her twenty-six years. She danced with the American Ballet Theatre at Lincoln Center in Manhattan at age six; became the published author of a children's book, *She Was Nice To*

Mice, at age twelve; and then went on to attend an exclusive Manhattan prep school, do TV commercials, and become a movie star before she was twenty.

But all wasn't perfect in Sheedy's life during this period. She developed a problem with bulimia during her teen years, and at times, she would become emaciated and totally fatigued when she should have been in top physical condition to pursue her many interests.

"I did a lot of work on myself to get through it," she told a *Parade* interviewer.[6]

There are a lot of different therapies and a lot of clinics you can go to. But it finally comes down to you. You have to be willing to change that sort of behavior, and it took me years to beat it. When you have an emotional disorder, you have to decide that you don't want your life being ruled by an obsession. And food is an obsession, whether you're gorging it or refusing it.

Today, Ally Sheedy seems to have put her achievements in better perspective. To be sure, she's still ambitious, still trying hard to improve and move ahead in her craft. But she has tried to head off any distortion of her success drive by focusing on

- good nutrition;
- avoidance of alcohol and drugs;
- use of relaxation techniques;
- involvement in her favorite political causes; and
- finishing her college degree.

She continues to hone her acting craft by working hard in drama workshops and taking voice lessons, but she took an extended break from performing in any new films during 1987 just to be sure that her life was moving forward at a healthy pace.

One person who apparently failed to slow down and gain some sense of balance in her career was Gelsey Kirkland, the youthful ballerina who joined the New York City Ballet at age fifteen and became the Sugar Plum Fairy in the Nutcracker Ballet. By age twenty-eight, according to her book *Dancing on My Grave* (New York: Doubleday, 1986), she had become involved in drug abuse, undergone a variety of silicone implants in her breasts, ankles, and hips, and tortured her body with radical diets and binge-and-vomit eating.

Kirkland's personal relationships, including her love life, were also unsatisfying during her ballet stardom. She had a falling out with George Balanchine, who ran the New York City Ballet, and she left that company to dance with Mikhail Baryshnikov at the American Ballet Theatre. But a love affair with Baryshnikov proved ill-fated, with each attacking the other in public as an inadequate sexual partner.

Now Kirkland is dancing with the Royal Ballet in London. Her experiences, which she catalogues in detail in her book, provide an object lesson on how individual career achievement, by itself, is incapable of providing satisfaction, a sense of balance, and inner peace.

Certainly not every woman who gets involved in the Success Cult and becomes addicted to the heady aroma of high achievement will necessarily lose her physical health, suffer serious emotional disorders, or find her personal relationships in shambles. But many will. These physical and emotional features of the Female Mistake, which echo similar problems faced by achievement-addicted men, should serve as a warning to all of us who are driven by a deep inner need to accomplish, acquire, or be the best.

Paranoia about Losing Personal Identity

Some women who are on the fast track live in a constant state of fear that they will lose their identity as high achievers if they get too close to a man. I've counseled numerous women who, in considering a marriage proposal, say they are reluctant to make a permanent matrimonial commitment because they are afraid they'll just become appendages of their husbands.

Some who finally decide to get married may try to attach all sorts of qualifications to the relationship. In some respects this attitude may reflect an effort to retain a clear-cut identity apart from a spouse. One such woman, who had established herself as a highly competent buyer in a major retail chain, walked into my office and laid out an entire laundry list of what I can only characterize as "demands" that her prospective husband would have to meet before she would deign to accept him. As I examined the list it became evident to me that each item reflected the fact that she hoped to give her personal identity—an identity wrapped up in her career—a priority over everything else, including marriage.

Specifically, she said she wanted
- a detailed prenuptial agreement, giving her (in the event of a divorce) the right to all her property and investments she brought to the marriage;

- a separate apartment, in case she needed to work in solitude or perhaps "get away" from the relationship for a time;
- an understanding that she frequently had to make trips out of town and entertain male clients—and her husband was not to get jealous or possessive when she had to perform these duties; and
- certain qualifications in the marriage vows so that she could be sure she would be treated as a completely equal partner in the arrangement.

This young woman was desperately afraid that she would become known as "the wife of" her husband, with the result that her identity, including her reputation in her field, might suffer. To assuage her fears the couple did eventually draft and sign a prenuptial agreement, and they also made some adjustments to the traditional marriage vows so that the wife would feel like an equal partner. Fortunately, she agreed to back off on some of her other demands, and I think that was a very healthy development.

Marriage, after all, is a bonding together of two different personalities, it *does* involve some merging of one person's identity and interests with the identity and interests of the spouse. Marriage should be entered into only with the understanding that the relationship is going to get a high priority in one's life—a priority that should be superseded only by allegiance to and commitment to God.

Yet in this case the young woman began with the assumption that her career came first. Only after considerable counseling and discussions with her fiance did she realize that she was not just asking for equality. She actually wanted her occupational interests to be given a priority over him and the relationship. When she finally understood the mistake she had been making, she was able to relax more, let her guard down, and trust in her husband's love and good intentions, just as he trusted in hers.

The Loss of Important Personal Values

Perhaps the most destructive feature of the Female Mistake is the potential for losing basic values. Sometimes women who desperately need to succeed may cut corners in the way they've been taught to treat people. For example, many people have been brought up to believe that gossiping about a person or "stabbing someone in the back" with false accusations or innuendo is reprehensible. Yet the desire to best a competitor may become overwhelming. Many otherwise principled working women have revealed to me, almost incidentally in conversations about problems they were having at work, that they had been bad-mouthing competitors with great success, but they obviously didn't feel quite right about it.

"The men in our company have an unfair advantage because they always stick together, back each other up and, more often than not, get the best promotions," one female executive told me.

So sometimes, I feel I have to redress the balance. I just drop a word here or an observation there about them to other colleagues or even to my superiors. I try not to seem catty—just concerned about the welfare of the organization. A few times this approach seems to have given me

an advantage. Most times it doesn't appear to have any effect at all. Other times, I'm sorry to say, my relationship with the people I've confided in seems to deteriorate.

On a pragmatic as much as on a moral basis, this woman decided not to continue with verbal guerrilla warfare against her colleagues. However, she had already tarnished her reputation and had established herself as something of a viper at work. Only when she moved to another company was she able to reassert her old moral values and establish herself as a more pleasant business companion.

Another area where a career woman's personal values may be placed in jeopardy involves her desire to have children, even though she's not married. One accomplished musician, who had forgone marriage in favor of pursuing her career, decided in her late thirties that she wanted to have a child. At the time she wasn't dating anyone she wanted to marry. She stopped using any contraceptive devices, began to have regular sex with two or three men she felt had "good genes," and finally became pregnant. This woman came from a family that stressed traditional morality, including having sex and children only within the marriage relationship. But her drive to have a successful career, without what she regarded as the "encumbrances" of marriage, caused her to ignore the moral values she had been taught and to go ahead and have a child out of wedlock. Not only that, she had the child without making an attempt to identify or notify the father!

I became aware of this situation when the woman made an appointment with me for what she said would have to be a "very confidential" discussion. She showed up with her mother and proceeded to tell both of us, for the first time, what she had done. She wanted to be sure, she said, that the baby would be baptized.

The mother, a proper New Englander, was mortified, and I must say, I was a little shocked, even though I had encountered similar cases. This situation was so surprising because I never would have expected this woman, whom I had known for a while, to take such a calculated step in contradiction to her moral upbringing. I had failed to anticipate the intoxicating, distorting influence that the drive for success can wield over those who give achievement the top priority in their lives.

These, then, are a few of the dangers and tragedies that may arise from what I've called the Female Mistake. Obviously, women, like men, can do many things to break their unhealthy addiction to achievement and find true success in their lives. So far we've already explored in some detail how anyone, man or woman, can find a more accurate and beneficial personal definition of success, stop trying to turn the job into a god, and learn to share success.

What other, distinctive considerations should the achievement-oriented woman keep in mind as she tries to get her life back on track? To answer this question, we'll look at some ways to correct the Female Mistake.

SOME SPECIAL RESPONSES TO THE FEMALE MISTAKE

If you're a woman who feels trapped or threatened in some way by the Success Cult, I'd suggest, in addition to following some of the other guidelines in this book, that you respond in these special ways to the challenge.

Special Response #1: Follow Your Personal Values and Intuitions, Not Those Promoted by the Success Cult.

Many of the distorted, addictive values of achievement have originally been established by men. Often without quite understanding what's happening to them, career-oriented women may get trapped by the same fallacious ways of believing, thinking, and acting. Like their male counterparts, these women don't stop to consider that perhaps the values of childhood or the values advocated by their religious faith are more valid than those they automatically affirm in pursuit of a successful career.

Recently, three young women—Jessica Hahn, Donna Rice, and Fawn Hall—gained notoriety because of their associations with the flawed behavior of some of our nation's well-known men. Far from turning their backs on these involvements, they decided to cash in on the celebrity status they achieved. Hahn posed half nude for *Playboy* and provided the magazine with a "tell-all" interview detailing her sexual encounter with TV evangelist Jim Bakker. Rice, the one-time weekend companion of presidential candi-

date Gary Hart, enlisted the help of a battery of law-
yers, literary agents, and other advisers. Her goal was
to gain further recognition and make money from
product endorsements, TV appearances, and other
sources. Hall, the blonde secretary for the Iran-Contra
spymaster Oliver North—though apparently the most
conservative and traditional of the group—signed up
with a major talent agency in an effort to launch a career as a TV newscaster.

Although the experiences of these three young
women are quite unusual because of the circumstances surrounding their swift achievement of notoriety, they illustrate the national tendency to respond
in almost knee-jerk reaction whenever any opportunity, regardless of its moral implications, is presented
to increase fame or financial status. Many people
never stop to ask, Is it really appropriate for me to cap-
italize on my current position? Is it right to exploit my
situation for money, fame, or other gain? Instead, they
try to get as much money and career mileage out of
the position that they can, though often what they gain
in the end is much less than they had hoped for or
expected.

As one *New York Times* analysis put it, "If the past
holds any clues about these three women's prospects
for enduring fame, their chances are not very good."[7]
This same article supported its thesis about the *un-
enduring* quality of this kind of success by citing such
flashes in the pan as Cristine Keeler (former lover of
John Profumo, British defense minister); Fanne Fox
(the "Argentine firecracker" and stripper who helped
bring down U.S. representative Wilbur D. Mills); Eliza-
beth Ray (secretary and paramour of U.S. representa-

tive Wayne Hays); and Rita Jenrette (who, as wife of a
U.S. representative, posed in the buff for *Playboy* and
gave interviews about congressional sexual escapades
to the press).

Clearly, neither these women nor the male role
models they may be following should be the standard.
Women, as well as men, need to be more independent-
minded about how they define and aspire to success.
They should evaluate the things they are asked to do
and pose more questions about the demands their careers often make of them. No woman should feel com-
pelled to change her beliefs or embrace questionable
actions just because there are male precedents for
pursuing false values on the road to success.

An excellent example of a woman who has stuck to
her guns in affirming her own values, not those of the
men around her, is Caroline Rose Hill, one of the heirs
of the great Texas-based fortune of the late H. L. Hunt.
Her three brothers—Nelson Bunker, William Herbert,
and Lamar—have recently gotten into financial hot
water because of their speculations in silver, sugar,
and oil. They reportedly owe creditors $2.43 billion,
but the liquidation value of their assets is only $1.48
billion. As a result they are currently involved in complex litigation, including a bankruptcy proceeding,
which is costing them $1 million a month.[8]

In contrast, Caroline Rose Hill (formerly known as
Caroline Hunt Schoellkopf, before her divorce) has
insisted on complete integrity in and conservative
management of her investments. She's managed to increase her part of the Hunt fortune rather than jeop-
ardize its existence. Her holdings hover at
approximately $1 billion, give or take a few million,

according to reports in *Fortune, Forbes*, and the *New York Times.*

So what does Caroline Hill's experience have to say to other women? Certainly, she's not a typical career woman. For one thing, she inherited her wealth. Also, she has more money than most women or men ever dream of. Moreover, she leaves the management of her money to trusted advisers and generally stays in the background in her business ventures. But no one would argue that Caroline Hill is an astute and palpable presence in establishing the values that control the management of her money. Despite any temptations or pressures she may have felt to take risks like her brothers, she has elected to follow her own light in the investment field, with spectacularly successful results.

Special Response #2: Pay Attention to Proper Timing As You Plan Your Life's Goals.

Women, even more than men, find life has a special pacing and timing, which they must observe carefully if they hope to stay on the path to true success. In particular, many women become concerned about balancing three major elements in their lives: their career, marriage, and children.

A career woman who really wants to get married and have children may find herself, almost perversely, devoting all her waking hours to her job. She has no time to date, much less meet a prospective mate, get married, and start a family. According to some recent statistics, if the average woman waits too long—say past her thirties—her chances of getting married decline precipitously.

So, as obvious as it may seem, many hard-driving women simply have to be told, "You know, if you want to get married, you'll have to put aside your ambition now and then and place yourself in a situation where you'll meet eligible men!"

I can recall one young woman in her late twenties, an investment counselor, who worked ten to twelve hours a day at her office and then returned home to fine tune the investment strategies of her clients on her home computer. She barely took time to eat, much less pursue an active social life. When she did go out for some recreation, it was always to the movies with one of her female friends. Yet she couldn't figure out why she was having trouble meeting marriageable men!

My advice to her: "Get involved with other young people in our parish. Help plan potluck lunches, attend Bible studies, and engage in other fellowship and social contacts." As I told her, the idea was not to plunge into these activities *only* to find a husband. Rather, she should try to broaden her friendships and, more important, her spiritual experience. Then the possibilities for meeting a mate would be more likely to follow. This was exactly what she did, and now she is at least involved in regular dating.

I would never advocate that women begin to frequent singles bars or otherwise make desperate attempts to find eligible men. There are many possibilities for increasing social contacts with reputable members of the opposite sex, such as in churches and synagogues, at professional association meetings, and at other social events.

By the same token, if a woman's career (or her career plus her marriage) becomes virtually the only important factor in her life, she may never find time to have children, at least not until it's too late. At this time, about thirty-three million women, who comprise 28 percent of the nation's potential work force, are of childbearing age. So an overwhelming number of career-oriented females are facing this problem of pacing and timing their lives so that they can fit it all in—*all* meaning a successful career, a marriage, *and* children.

Don't allow your career to prevent you from making choices about marriage and children. I'd suggest that you do what one career woman I know did. Try plugging career success, marriage, and children into an overall plan for your life. Then, as best you can, pace yourself so as to maximize your chances to achieve all your personal goals.

One woman recognized early that some factors in her life were more or less fixed. She could have children only up to a certain biologically determined age. Also, although there are exceptions, she acknowledged that her chances to get married would probably decrease as she got older. Even though she started her career in law immediately after she graduated from law school and passed the bar, she didn't allow her work to take a priority over marriage.

As it happened, she met and fell in love with a young man in law school. They decided to get married immediately, although both of them realized tremendous demands would be placed on them at work in their first years as legal associates. Furthermore, they both had to accept jobs in the same city if they hoped to be able to spend any time together. In effect, despite the pressures on them, this couple gave marriage at least equal billing with their careers, and their relationship worked well because each spouse was sympathetic to the work demands of the other.

But how could they fit children into this scenario? It took some planning.

The law firm where the wife worked was sympathetic to providing an extended maternal leave to new mothers. So after about four years, when the wife had established herself as a valuable associate, the couple had the first of their two children. She took two months off to be sure that the nanny they hired would work out, and she was back in her office shortly afterward. Two years later she went through the same routine with their second child. The entire sequence of events was completed by the time she was thirty-four.

I'll acknowledge there are many potential problems in trying to pull off such a balancing act with a high-powered career, a marriage, and children. But so far—and several years have passed—this woman is succeeding with considerable aplomb.

Other women I know have worked out satisfying variations on this theme. One woman married and launched a career almost simultaneously. But she waited until she was in her midthirties to have her first and only child, at which time she had reached the upper echelons of her field.

Feeling a strong need to be a full-time mother, she quit her job completely for several years until her son was school age and away from home most of the day. At that point she took up her career again. However, she made certain that she, her husband, or a trusted nanny was always present to take the child to school and pick him up.

Women, more than men, often feel a need to go through these scheduling acrobatics because, traditionally, the burden of child rearing has been placed on their shoulders. These days, as fathers become more involved with their children, some of this burden is being eased in many families. But it's likely that career women who want it all will have to continue to pay very close attention to timing the big commitments in their lives if they hope to achieve true and satisfying success.

Special Response #3: Put Yourself in a Position to Give and Receive Encouragement.

Women who are trying to succeed in a big way in the working world are in many ways trailblazers. Women in past eras succeeded in traditional careers, such as teaching and nursing. For the most part, though, men dominated business, government, and the professions, and it's only been in recent years that significant numbers of women have appeared on the scene to challenge the dominance of men in these areas.

Perhaps as a result of this relative newness of the career involvement of women, or maybe because some are uncertain whether their sense of identity should be derived primarily from the home or the working world, many women who come to me display a severe lack of self-confidence. Men, of course, often have the same difficulty. But the problem seems more prevalent in women these days, and I find they are in particular need of encouragement and nurturance. Without such emotional support many end up failing at their jobs, their marriages, and motherhood, mainly because they begin to believe that they're somehow inherently unable to perform.

In one recent study of the lack of achievement among black female students, two University of Florida researchers concluded that the girls' problems arose from a failure of their teachers to encourage them in intellectual pursuits. The researchers found that teachers from kindergarten through third grade praised white females for academic behavior, but they usually only praised the blacks for helping other children with personal or emotional problems. As the children got older, the black females became more socially isolated, their sense of self-esteem apparently decreased, and their academic performance declined in relation to that of the other students.

In light of such studies and also my own observations of female adults over the years, I always advise young career women to seek out companions who will build them up rather than tear them down. Too often both men and women will inadvertently allow themselves to slip into a negative mode of thinking, and the source of the problem can often be traced to the fact that their usual companions are relatives, friends, or colleagues who emphasize the minuses rather than the pluses of life.

One writer who began her career with a prominent literary agent found that he was always telling her what she was doing wrong instead of what she was doing right. "No, no, I can't possibly sell this book proposal!" he would say. Or "Those sample chapters just aren't up to professional quality. Try again!"

Unfortunately, he didn't offer any *constructive* criticism. He wouldn't try to tell her what she was doing wrong so that she could take steps to correct the problem. Despite the nay saying, this woman managed to be published in several magazines and even had a book accepted for publication. But the negative influence of her agent finally got her down. He would occasionally drop hints that she wasn't as talented as his other clients and that her potential was so limited that perhaps she should consider another field.

Her morale suffered so much that she couldn't turn out enough publishable material to make a living. In desperation she turned to another agent, and that turned out to be the best decision of her life. This man, in contrast to her first representative, began in an upbeat way to tell her how "talented" she was and "what a great future" she was going to have with him. Almost overnight the quality of her work improved.

Today, she is a top free-lance author with more work than she can handle, and she is recognized by dozens of people in the publishing industry as one of the most gifted writers around. But the key to her success was that she finally placed herself in a position where her self-confidence was strengthened.

With these and similar responses, the career-oriented woman can begin to develop the tools she needs to overcome the Female Mistake and avoid following the men around her into the fallacies and addictions of the Success Cult.

CHAPTER NINE

THE GREAT RULE OF RESTLESSNESS

In his *Confessions,* St. Augustine said, "Our hearts are restless 'til they find their rest in Thee." One of the many variations on this theme is a restlessness that often accompanies significant human achievement.

In every career and especially at high levels of accomplishment, many people report a gnawing urge to "do more," "find new frontiers to conquer," or "move on to something else." Whatever they achieve somehow fails to satisfy; whatever they accomplish somehow lacks the power to bring a sense of completion or having "arrived." Even when the accomplishments have been impressive by outward standards, these achievers have a feeling of having fallen short of true success.

This Rule of Restlessness, as I call it, can have some of its most disturbing effects on people at the very highest levels of achievement. For example, winners of major prizes like the Nobel, Pulitzer, or Academy Award may report an inexplicable emptiness, disappointment, or anxiety in addition to their positive feelings. Here's a sampling of such reactions from a study cited in the *New York Times:*[1]

Arno Penzias, winner of the 1978 Nobel for physics: "People inside tend to feel a little fraudulent, and winning the Nobel Prize highlights that feeling. You see your own shortcomings, not those of others."

Playwright Lanford Wilson, winner of the 1980 Pulitzer, on writer's block after winning: "Type 'This is the next play by last year's Pulitzer Prize winner' at the top of a page and try to write something underneath it."

I. I. Rabi, winner of the Nobel in physics in 1944: "Unless you are very competitive, you aren't likely to function with the same vigor afterward."

Earl W. Wallace, winner of an Academy Award for his screenplay for the movie *Witness:* "I have an uneasy feeling my career just peaked."

F. Murray Abraham, winner of an Academy Award for his role in *Amadeus:* "The fact is that the anxieties I had were replaced by new anxieties."

J. Anthony Lukas, winner of two Pulitzers: "Of course I wanted to win one very badly, and once I had it, there was this letdown. [I thought] 'What am I going to do with the rest of my life? Can I find something that I'm obsessed about?' And there was a kind of panic that I would never

find something that I would care so much about."

In a similar vein, the movie actor Kirk Douglas, a household name and certainly someone most people would regard as a success, confided, "In a sense, I feel like a failure because I've never attained what I wanted to do in life: I wanted to be a star on the Broadway stage."[2]

One of the most resounding successes in the entertainment industry in recent years has been George Lucas, who with his *Star Wars* trilogy and other film work has almost single-handedly transformed the look of the movies. By all outward signs Lucas has achieved a great deal. Yet he seems to have been plagued by the Rule of Restlessness.

After making a personal fortune of about $50 million on the *Star Wars* movies, he lost most of it in a divorce proceeding. He also came under such pressure from fans and fanatics alike that he retreated from the public arena and became a virtual recluse.

"That kind of success is very difficult to deal with, very disruptive to one's personal life," he told a *New York Times* reporter. "It took eight years and a lot of creative energy and emotional torment to complete the movies. Then the divorce. Divorce is a very difficult thing financially and emotionally. I went into a several-year tailspin."[3]

The problems posed by the Rule of Restlessness, which tends to have the most devastating impact on those who have achieved many or most of their earthly goals, also affect many top-level athletes. Greg Louganis, who has won two Olympic gold medals for diving, as well as awards for many other major international diving championships, once said, "Less than winning means I failed."[4]

After Louganis finished in second place three times in one meet, he told his coach, "I'm doubting myself. I don't have faith in my abilities at this point."

His coach, Ron O'Brien, replied, "Well, then, if you don't have faith in yourself, have faith in me. I'll stand by you. We'll get through this together."

The result? Louganis proceeded to win several firsts in his next two meets.

Another outwardly successful person is Pam Shriver, the tennis pro, who has won more than $2 million in tournament play since 1978. She also owns a tennis club and has other valuable real estate investments. Still, Shriver often doubts herself:

> **Sometimes, I wonder whether I'm cut out to be a tennis player. Sometimes, I feel as if I'm in prison and I have to stay for another six or seven years. Sometimes, I'm so frustrated, so enraged, so discouraged that I'd like to run away and hide. . . . The pressure of feeling high expectations is crippling.**[5]

And then there's John McEnroe. Called by at least one sports writer "one of the best tennis players the planet has ever seen," McEnroe sometimes seems the epitome of restlessness and frustration in the midst of supersuccess. You'd think that a man who has won most of the world's major titles, including Wimbledon and the U.S. Open, would feel as though he were on top of the world. But "McNasty" or "McBrat," as the members of the press have called him, has probably shown more unhappiness and thrown more tantrums on the court than any other player in history.

When he lost unexpectedly in the quarterfinals at Wimbledon in 1985, he was already feeling burned-out and washed-up. "I didn't feel as fresh as I like out there today," he told a *New York Times* writer. "I felt a little old. I know 26 is not old age, but I've been on the tour eight years, and at times, it catches up to you."[6]

That was a mild reaction. One of the most explosive occurred at the 1987 U.S. Open, where he cursed the umpire mercilessly after a disputed call: "Couldn't you see the ——— call? That cost me the ——— set. ——— you! You ———!" Then McEnroe launched a tirade against a TV sound man.

As a result of his outbursts, McEnroe was fined $5,000 for verbally abusing the umpire, $2,000 for cursing the sound man, and $500 for unsportsman-like conduct. Furthermore, because of an accumulation of other fines, he faced an additional $10,000 penalty and a two-month suspension. As shocking as McEnroe's behavior sometimes is, however, he's just showing he's subject to the same Rule of Restlessness that has caused less emotional achievers to react in milder and perhaps more socially acceptable ways.

How, exactly, does this sense of dissatisfaction and restlessness emerge in an achiever's life? What personal characteristics and personal flaws foster the discontent? What, if anything, can you do to prevent the Rule of Restlessness from becoming an unpleasant reality in your life?

THE ROOTS OF THE RULE
OF RESTLESSNESS

Based on my observations of a wide variety of achievers at different stages of their careers, I've concluded that the Rule of Restlessness doesn't usually become a serious reality until an individual has reached some significant level of achievement. I'm not saying the Rule won't apply until you've attained one or all of your ultimate goals in life. However, you have to be far enough along in your career to begin to ask, What is this all about? What am I working so hard for? Why don't my accomplishments give me any more satisfaction? It's at this point of high or reasonably high achievement that the restlessness, discontent, doubt, or anxiety is most likely to set in.

To help you understand in practical terms how this phenomenon may arise, I'd like to introduce you to two high achievers: a land baron and a major church leader, who at least began to approach true success. But both found the inner fruits of achievement snatched from their grasp by the great waves of restlessness that swept over them.

The Land Baron
A major real estate magnate, who had made his fortune in all sorts of commercial land deals in the Midwest, decided he had earned all the money he needed. He felt the time had arrived to accomplish some good with his millions. So he, his wife, and children moved to New York City where he took a position in a charitable organization he had helped to establish and support with his contributions.

This man (I'll call him Fred) had never known fail-ure in his life. He had inherited a substantial amount of money from his father, but through his own talents, he had increased the size of the family fortune many times over. He was highly respected socially, both in the Midwest and on the East Coast, and he had close ties to a major Christian denomination and was gener-ally regarded as an influential churchman.

I got to know him because he was interested in in-fusing considerable amounts of money to help the down-and-out urban dwellers, including many of the homeless and drug addicts. For his philanthropic work he received national and international awards— so many, in fact, that sometimes it seemed he was spending most of his time being honored by domestic and foreign dignitaries!

As I learned through my contacts with him, how-ever, Fred was not a happy man. He had trouble main-taining close, intimate relationships. He and his wife were divorced soon after they arrived in New York. Also, Fred remained extremely competitive and achievement-oriented, even after he had made his mil-lions and received more honors than he could display on his walls. He even told me he woke up every morn-ing by exclaiming, "Lord, give me another day of peak performance!"

But this wasn't a joyous prayer, nor was Fred a joy-ous person. Indeed, he may have been the most rest-less person I've ever met. Always demanding more of himself, of others, and of various institutions than could possibly be delivered, he remained constantly frustrated. He seemed to be chasing a pot of gold at the end of some rainbow that kept vanishing or shifting just as the prize seemed to come within his grasp.

Then Fred was struck by a terminal illness. He was devastated by the news, and he seemed to have a desperate need to work out some of his unresolved religious beliefs before the end came. So he asked me to meet regularly with him during his remaining months.

As we pursued our discussions it became evident that he was motivated, not by a biblical faith, but by a humanist vision, reinforced to some extent by Christian imagery and concepts. Specifically, he believed in the ultimate power of human social movements and of the political process to bring about a kind of heaven on earth.

"The kingdom of God doesn't involve some ethereal life after death," he told me one evening. "The kingdom begins and ends right on this earth, and it's up to us to usher it in."

I told him I didn't quite see things that way. "Sure, God wants us to do everything we can to promote justice and help the poor and oppressed," I said. "But all Christian ethics and values begin with the death and resurrection of Jesus Christ. Everything we believe or do on this earth will ultimately be judged after we die in light of one ultimate reference point—our personal relationship with Christ."

Fred wasn't convinced. Even though he could see the limits of his human powers (after all, he was dying of cancer), he wasn't willing to acknowledge that he had lost control over his life. He continued to search vainly for the answers to life's problems in his money, his social connections, and the powerful friends he had cultivated.

But it was all to no avail. The sicker he got, the more restless, frustrated, and depressed he became. He lashed out at what he called the inferior people in the church, the government, and business. He seemed to believe that if he could somehow wake people up and get them motivated, they would become as committed to excellence as he was. Then suddenly, the sorry state of the world would take a turn for the better.

Unfortunately, Fred died before he gained a clear understanding of where he had gone wrong. He had been looking only to himself and to the values associated with human achievement to answer the deepest questions of life. But this approach was doomed to failure from the very start. Because of his high demands and expectations, people and their institutions always disappointed him.

Certainly, he saw some progress and some benefits in the increased material well-being of the poor people he tried to help, but in every case, things didn't improve enough to suit him. He had developed unrealistic expectations of what people were capable of and had lost his sense of perspective on what should be important in this life. Instead of cultivating a relationship with God, he chose to try to *become* God in his dealings with those less fortunate than himself. But he found that despite his many gifts, the job of overseeing and remaking God's world was far beyond his meager human capacities.

Fred passed away a frustrated and unhappy man. The memory of his life continues to pain me because I don't believe he understood why his great achievements ultimately failed to satisfy him or bring him inner peace.

The Major Church Leader

Many lay people think that church leaders understand a great deal about spiritual development and about the best uses of the power of faith. But that is not always the case.

One high-ranking church leader who has enjoyed all the privileges of a good education, social connections, and respect from his community, has gained a wide reputation as a powerful preacher and writer on causes designed to improve the living conditions and political power of people in Third World countries. Sometimes he gets so agitated about foreigners' rights he feels are being violated that he'll viciously attack anyone who even suggests that there may be another side to the positions he espouses.

Of course, those who agree with this leader's views regard him as a great and anointed leader. He has gained wide recognition in many segments of the news media as a respected spokesperson for his viewpoints.

Despite the outward signs of success and achievement, this church leader has some serious problems in his inner life and personal relationships. He reflects the working of the Rule of Restlessness because even though he achieves much of what he sets out to do, he never seems to experience any sense of joy or contentment. He often accomplishes some goal or political objective, but he focuses on the little failures and things that go wrong. Then he gets frustrated and takes out his discontent on his coworkers and family members.

One important source of his restlessness is his misguided self-reliance. Even though he's been taught to look to God for his support, he usually looks only to himself. His reaction to most of his accomplishments is to point to what *he's* been able to do, not what God has been able to do through him.

Also, this churchman tends to neglect forming close personal relationships in favor of promoting movements and projects on a national and international scale. He tries to uphold the rights and welfare of people in general instead of people as individuals. As a result he often runs roughshod over those closest to him, such as his staff, his colleagues, his friends, and even his family. In his view it's not acceptable for any individual to take priority over the cause, whatever that cause may be at the moment.

I'm not suggesting that we should neglect participating in social causes or helping those in faraway lands. On the contrary, I believe in promoting such causes vigorously, with all the resources available. But at the same time I believe we should also give a top priority to our relationships with those who are closest to us. Certainly, that was the way Jesus operated. He devoted most of His time on this earth to (1) His relationship with God the Father; (2) His relationships with His disciples, close friends, and loved ones; (3) and His encounters with individuals who approached Him with some specific need.

This major church leader has allowed his basic priorities to get out of order. He's lost perspective on what true success and satisfying achievement are all about.

Clearly, the farther you move up the ladder of achievement, the more vulnerable you become to the great Rule of Restlessness, which can rob you of the joy, satisfaction, and peace that every high achiever regards as his birthright. Is there any way to escape this unhappy condition? There is if you'll learn to replace the Rule of Restlessness with the Rule of Life.

THE RULE OF LIFE:
THE ULTIMATE ANSWER
TO RESTLESSNESS

Throughout Christian history most believers who have wanted to draw as close as possible to God have followed in some sense what I call a Rule of Life. Sometimes, the Rule has been formal, as with a number of monastic orders. St. Benedict's Rule, which outlines times for prayer, sleep, work, and other daily activities, is one example of this formal approach.

On the other hand, many Christians who have not become involved in a formal order or organized brotherhood or sisterhood have, over the years, formulated their own rules. This less formal, more individualized approach is what I'm suggesting here, in part because I've found my personal Rule of Life to be an invaluable guide. Without my special Rule of Life, I feel certain that I would become extremely vulnerable to the restlessness that often accompanies the worldly drive to success.

What, specifically, is involved in formulating a Rule of Life? It should have two main purposes. First, you should use it to project your vision of what you want to happen in your life, what you want your priorities to be, and how you hope to achieve them. Second, you should rely on the Rule to chronicle on a regular basis

THE GREAT RULE OF RESTLESSNESS

how you've been doing in achieving your ultimate goals and ordering your personal priorities.

In my case, I decided first of all that I wanted to be sure my life was sufficiently ordered and disciplined so that I would have time to pursue the following important interests and responsibilities:

- Bible reading
- prayer and reflection
- study and intellectual preparation, both for my preaching and also for my general awareness of current events and trends
- family life
- my work and ministry

Initially, in my journal, I jotted down these broad categories, which I regarded as important in determining how I would use my time. Then I outlined in more detail how I would achieve these goals.

For example, I decided that my commitment to prayer would involve both private prayer and corporate prayer. So I set aside about a half-hour a day just to talk to God. Sometimes I pray at home; or sometimes I continue my conversations with God in a subway, in a taxicab, or on a city street.

To experience corporate prayer, I've joined a small prayer group that meets every day in one of our church buildings. We gather for about ten to fifteen minutes, Monday through Friday, and follow certain traditional forms of praying and reading the Scriptures. Although I don't serve as leader of the group very often, I've found it to be invaluable in helping me get each day started with God at the forefront of my thinking. Also, I meet once a week for a prayer-and-share time with some Christians who have been involved, as I have, in the Cursillo Movement, a spiritual renewal force in several of the major denominations.

To help me study regularly, I've joined a reading club, consisting of a group of clergy who meet once a month to discuss books they've read. Sometimes the books are on theology, sometimes on history, and other times on a current topic. Also, I try to read the *New York Times* regularly, just to be certain that my preaching and witnessing remain relevant and show a familiarity with current events and thought. As the Protestant theologian Karl Barth once said, preachers should speak with the Bible in one hand and the newspaper in the other!

Finally, I try to spend plenty of time with my wife and my children. It's so easy, with all the other activities and obligations of life, to allow a week to breeze by without spending some prime or quality time with my wife. For me that kind of time means private, in-depth conversation and communication, not just being in the same general location at the same party, church event, or family gathering.

As for my children, I try to see the older ones regularly, even though they're away from home now more often than they're with us. But my youngest, Nicholas, is around all the time, and like any six-year-old, he presents special challenges because of his high energy levels—and my tendency to be tired or preoccupied when I arrive home at night. It's so easy to be negative rather than positive with such an active youngster. It's so easy to say, "Get your feet off the table!" It takes much more effort to engage a young child in meaningful, positive communication that interests him as well as me.

As far as my work is concerned, my Rule of Life commits me to fulfill my responsibilities as well as I can and still keep my spiritual and family life intact. Moreover, strange as this may sound coming from a minister, I find I have to pray that I'll be able to focus consistently on the *human* dimensions of my work instead of just on tasks and projects. A high percentage of what I do is concerned more with running a small corporation—tending to property, finances, and personnel systems—than with developing personal interactions with individuals. As a result I have to rely heavily on God to help my humanize my work and keep my priorities in order.

I try as hard as I can to maintain some sort of balance with my spiritual life, my family life, and my work. Yet I suspect that without my Rule of Life, it would be easy for many of my family relationships to fall by the wayside because my loved ones don't put the same kind of demands, pressures, and deadlines on me that my work does.

To monitor myself so as to be sure that my Rule of Life is a vital guide and presence in daily existence, I rely on a journal, feedback from one of the prayer groups I attend, and the advice of a spiritual director. In the journal I keep a list of each of the important points in my Rule. On a fairly regular basis I'll jot down my feelings and my evaluation of how I'm faring in my development. Also, the weekly prayer-and-share group I attend is oriented toward helping the members with their spiritual development. I may report to them on some successes or failures in my life and then ask for their advice and prayer. Finally, I meet regularly with a mature Christian friend, to whom I've

given permission to be tough with me when he per-
ceives a failing I need to correct.

This briefly summarizes my Rule of Life. I must say
that I've found this approach invaluable for keeping
my life, including my ambition and drive for success,
in better balance. There was a time, about ten years
ago, when I didn't live according to such a Rule, and at
that time, I was much more inclined to let my priorities get out of whack. My work might take over my life
to the extent that my family commitments got completely pushed out of the picture. Or my work and
family might loom as so important that my spiritual
life, including my times alone with God, fell into neglect.

But the situation changes when you actually commit yourself to a Rule, write it down, and then monitor
yourself. With a Rule you're much more likely to keep
your priorities in order. And with proper priorities, especially those regarding your relationship with God
and your family, you're much less likely to feel rest-
less, anxious, or otherwise out of sorts. The Rule of
Restlessness becomes irrelevant when the Rule of Life
is in control.

CHAPTER TEN

THE FINAL TESTS OF TRUE SUCCESS

I'm not sure anyone can, or should, be such a total success that there's nothing left to shoot for, no other dreams or fantasies to give flavor and excitement to life. True success, far from being a final goal that you can attain or acquire, is more dynamic. It's a developing attitude characterized by a special kind of personal balance, an inner sense of well-being accompanied by some significant outward achievement.

Certainly, you can't be a success without accomplishing something significant. But what is significant to one person may be relatively inconsequential to another. For example, many professional and business people can't imagine being successful unless they (1) rise to the upper echelons of their companies, (2) become widely recognized in their lifetimes as leading experts in their fields, and (3) earn incomes well into the six-figure range. By that definition, however, Mother Teresa of Calcutta wouldn't be successful because she doesn't earn a six-figure income. Few musicians, writers, or actors would be considered successful because they don't hold high positions in companies or organizations. And a person who remains unknown by society during his lifetime but whose work comes to light after his death would have to be judged something less than a success.

As much as we may want to succeed, we must acknowledge that success, in the last analysis, is a highly subjective concept. So it's essential that each person develop a Rule of Life that gauges success rather than rely on the standards or dictates of others. Once the Rule is established, priorities can be organized to lead toward an ultimate objective. But how can we tell if we're on the right track to true success?

To check my personal direction and progress, I rely on five final test questions to ask myself at regular intervals. This way I can be more sure I'm doing all I can to move toward true success.

THE FIVE FINAL TESTS OF TRUE SUCCESS

Test #1: Am I a Single-minded Hard Worker?

The book of Proverbs is full of advice and admonitions about the importance of working hard and being persistent in pursuing occupational responsibilities. Listen, for example, to these words of the biblical sage: "A slothful man will not catch his prey, but the diligent man will get precious wealth";[1] and "In all toil there is profit, but mere talk tends only to want."[2]

These words, though uttered millennia ago by Solomon and other Hebrew wise men who lived in a very different world from our own, still apply to us today. If you work hard and persistently over a lifetime, you'll most likely see a payoff in terms of some sort of achievement. On the other hand, if you don't work hard, you probably won't receive any payoff.

When asked what single factor was most important in their success at work, a group of corporate vice presidents surveyed by Korn-Ferry International put "hard work" at the top of their list.[3] Similarly, achievers listed in Marquis's *Who's Who* responded to a Gallup Poll question asking what personal characteristics or traits they believed had contributed to their success, and 70 percent of those responding cited the most important trait as "being a hard worker."[4]

This principle of hard work has been a key factor in the careers of high achievers in a wide variety of fields, from the entertainment industry to computer sales. Here are just a few illustrations that have recently come to my attention:

Actor *Paul Newman* described himself as a "terrier" because none of his achievements have ever come easily for him. He's had to work hard and persevere, often for many years, before he achieved his goals in life.

"I tried skiing for 10 years," he told the *New York Times Magazine*. "The only thing I ever felt graceful at was racing a car, and that took me 10 years to learn."[5]

Actress *Jane Alexander*, who has fought all her life to get decent female film roles, said about her career, "I never saw myself doing anything else. I have a lot of perseverance and an ability to take rejection."[6]

Japanese marketing executive *Seiji Miwa* of the Topre Corporation in Tokyo spent nine years of hard, constant work—four of them in the United States— trying virtually single-handedly to set up a successful sales operation in this country. Finally, in 1985, purchasing managers from NCR Corporation told him they would order fifteen hundred computer keyboards from him.

Miwa immediately called his home office and said simply, "Atta!" ("We got it!") His colleagues' response: "Omodeto gozaimasu!" ("Congratulations!")[7]

Still, hard work is only one of the major tests for success. Moreover, if you emphasize hard work exclusively, you may become a workaholic, and your excessive diligence and persistence may backfire. There are even indications that increasing numbers of corporations and executives are *insisting* that their staff members take vacations and reduce their long hours to prevent possible burnout.[8] So I find it essential to apply some other tests as I try to determine whether I'm really on the road to true success.

Test #2: Do I Face My Failures and Weaknesses Head-on?

The TV personality Hugh Downs has admitted that one of his greatest weaknesses was a sense of fear. "It's something I've had to deal with all my life," he told a *Parade* magazine reporter. "I was always full of fear. First, I was a terribly timid child. When I started out in radio, I had a murderous case of mike fright, and then, on television, of camera fright. I discovered that there's only one way to handle fear: Go out and scare yourself!"[9]

Downs decided to seek out risky situations, face them head-on, and deal with them directly rather than run from them. So he's tried flying a glider, driving a racing car at 175 miles per hour, scuba diving on Australia's Great Barrier Reef, diving in search of a lost Spanish galleon, and riding a killer whale around the pool at San Diego's Sea World. Also, Downs has sailed the Pacific from Panama to Tahiti, and he once helped rescue a friend who had fallen into a crevasse during an expedition to the South Pole.

I don't necessarily recommend this approach as you try to deal with your fears or other weaknesses, but I do think that Downs's method has something to commend it. I know I sometimes fear that my human motives will override God's will in certain situations. When that happens I have to deal directly with my concerns and do everything I can to avoid ignoring them.

For example, I want very much for my parish to be on a solid financial footing. For that to happen members of the parish must give generously while they are alive and also through bequests in their wills. But there are times when I'm placed in positions of potential conflict, such as when I'm counseling a person who has a terminal illness and who at the same time wants advice about how to dispose of property through a will.

"I'm in a real quandary," one elderly woman told me. "I don't have any close relatives, and I want to give a substantial part of my estate to the church. But I really don't understand wills and bequests that well. Also, I don't have the foggiest idea of how much money the church needs. Can you help me?"

Her plea placed *me* in a quandary too. Obviously, I knew that the church needed money, but I also knew that this woman needed a sympathetic ear and good, solid pastoral support during her last months of life.

Yet how could I strike a balance between these interests? Was it possible for one person to resolve the apparent conflict?

Since I was the only one available to help this woman make her decision, I explained my difficulty to her directly: "Look, I'm in a potential conflict here, and I want you to understand exactly what my problem is. Yes, the church does need money. Maintaining millions of dollars' worth of landmark property in Manhattan is an expensive business, and we never have enough to do the job we feel we should do. Also to fund our programs for the homeless, the hungry, and the spiritually needy, we have to have financial support.

"At the same time, though, I'm mainly concerned about you and your welfare. I'm your pastor, no matter what you decide, and quite frankly, you'd make things easier for me if you just said, 'Tom, I'm not going to give the church any money.'

"In any event, I can't make your decision for you. I know you have other charities you're interested in, and you'll have to balance their needs against ours. Also, you say you don't have any close relatives, but I know you have some close friends. Perhaps they are in need of some of the money you'll be leaving behind."

In other words, I first tried to let this woman see exactly what problems and conflicts I was experiencing. I disclosed my weaknesses and inadequacies to her, just as I acknowledged them to myself. Then I felt more comfortable giving her pastoral counsel and accepting the final decision she made about her estate.

On the other hand, if we ignore our weaknesses, conflicts, and failings, we'll never be in a position to experience progress. We'll never be able to move steadily toward true success.

Test #3: Do I Live by the Day and Tackle My Challenges One Step at a Time?

Jesus said in the Sermon on the Mount, "Therefore do not worry about tomorrow, for tomorrow will worry about its own things. Sufficient for the day is its own trouble."[10] Another way of putting the biblical thought might go like this: "Live by the day! Take care of your responsibilities one at a time!"

I recall one extremely talented and intelligent young man who in his early twenties decided that he wanted to be president of a billion-dollar corporation. There was nothing inherently wrong with this ambition, except for one thing: This fellow found he could think of nothing else, except the power and money he would control twenty or thirty years into the future. He fantasized about how he would put together huge deals with other corporations; how he would fly all around the world in his private jet; and how he would dispense his huge income to the needy in this country and abroad.

Unfortunately, this young man literally put the cart before the horse, and he failed to get his career moving in the direction he intended. He daydreamed so much about what he was going to do in the future that he neglected to pay attention to the obligations of the present. As a result, as smart as he was, he performed poorly in his graduate courses in business. Consequently, the top companies weren't interested in hiring him when he graduated. After he finally got a job, he acquired the reputation of being distracted and un-

reliable because, once again, he was constantly fanta-
sizing about his future rather than focusing on the
here and now.

When he finally came to me to discuss his problem,
he was already in his early thirties; he had lost two
good jobs; and he was far off the track that leads to
true success. In many ways his values seemed appropriate and his priorities were in order. Among other
things, he acknowledged the importance of his relationship with God and with his family. He devoted a
fair amount of time to spiritual disciplines and to his
wife and two children. But this man had failed to pass
the test of taking life one step at a time—and his failure had met with near-disastrous results.

Fortunately, after counseling him, he immediately
recognized what he had been doing wrong, and as
hard as it was, he made a concerted effort to ignore
entirely what *might* happen in the future. Instead, he
concentrated more on what *was* happening in the
present. Today he seems to be in the process of becoming a more effective and successful person.

One of the best role models I've encountered for this
particular one-step-at-a-time test is Donald Seibert,
the former CEO of the J.C. Penney Company. In his
book *The Ethical Executive,* Seibert says that he
always tried to live by these words of Jesus, "Do not
worry about tomorrow."

He started out as a shoe salesman; next, he became
an assistant store manager; then, a store manager.
Gradually, step by step, he worked his way up to the
very top of the multibillion-dollar J.C. Penney hierarchy.

But Seibert never allowed himself to look beyond

the next rung on the corporate ladder. At various points he thought, *Hmm, I think I might be able to handle my boss's job.* But as a junior or middle-level manager, he never thought, *I think I'll shoot for CEO.*

Because he always kept his mind on the job at hand, Seibert concentrated most of his energies on doing each assignment that was given to him to the best of his ability. As a result he quickly gained a reputation as a productive, competent, and reliable worker—an employee who could handle the next job up on the corporate ladder.

Test #4: Am I Living by My Rule of Life?

Your Rule of Life, as we've already seen, helps you evaluate and establish your personal priorities. It's essential to have a clear idea of and commitment to what must come first, second, and third in your life. If you don't, you'll find yourself getting confused, disorganized, and decidedly unsuccessful. Far too often highly gifted men and women fail to make the best use of their abilities because some important aspect of their lives careens out of control.

But even after you've settled upon a Rule of Life, it's essential to continue to monitor your performance by it. One man who drew up a Rule of Life decided that the principles had become such a part of him that he really didn't need to monitor himself so closely any more. He had been in the habit of checking every day or two to be sure that he was

- spending at least several hours a week with his wife and children;
- devoting at least eight hours a week to outside service to others; and

- spending a half-hour to an hour a day in private prayer and Bible reading.

He became so confident that he stopped keeping track of the time he was spending in these activities. He said, "I want to be sure that I'm not becoming legalistic" in following this Rule.

For a while things went along well for him. He had established some solid habits that continued for a month or more without his needing to pay particular attention to them. But then other demands of life began to intrude, and gradually, the time he had originally planned to spend with his family, with God in his devotions, and with the needy in service was squeezed out.

"Somehow, my life seems out of control," he told me one day. "I can't figure it out. I have a good job and seem to be doing well at it. My family's healthy and appears to be doing well. I can't put my finger on anything that's really obviously wrong. In fact, most things seem very right. But still, I'm too anxious and snappy with other people, and in general, I feel out of sorts."

By all outward measurements, this man was successful, and his future at work and with his loved ones seemed bright and even enviable. Yet he lacked a sense of equanimity and inner peace. So I asked some pointed, loaded questions because I knew he tried to live by a Rule of Life.

"How's your prayer life?"

He thought for a moment. "I go to church regularly, and I pray there."

"I'm not talking about that," I replied. "I know you

put a high value on private prayer. How much time have you been spending alone with God?"

"Not much."

"And how about your family? I know you say they're doing well, but how much *quality* time have you been spending with your wife and children?"

"Not enough," he replied honestly.

As we talked further, he acknowledged that he still believed in the Rule of Life he had established for himself. But he also admitted that he had stopped monitoring his consistency in living by his Rule.

Everyone needs to continue to monitor those commitments about priorities and values. If we try to let things take care of themselves, we'll discover they *won't* take care of themselves! A life unattended to or unsupervised by important principles and values will quickly degenerate into a life out of control.

Please understand that I'm not advocating some sort of rigid, legalistic structure for your life, where there's little leeway for free, spontaneous action or creativity. What I'm talking about is *discipline*.

The early Christians who responded to Peter's first sermon at Pentecost displayed a great deal of spiritual and personal freedom as they healed the sick, prophesied, and spoke in new, strange languages. But the new converts, as well as the older believers, also paid close attention to developing vital spiritual disciplines.

Specifically, the book of Acts tells us they observed four essential disciplines: (1) prayer; (2) listening to the apostles' teaching; (3) worship (the "breaking of the bread," or Communion); and (4) fellowship.[11] Without these disciplines, they would have failed to nurture their relationship with Christ, and inevitably, their faith would have fallen apart.

We need to exercise our spiritual and moral freedoms within a framework of discipline and of well-thought-out spiritual and moral principles. The Rule of Life becomes a reference point to remind us of the living reality of God and of the values He wants us to incorporate in our lives.

Test #5: Do I Have Sufficient Faith?

Ultimately, any test of success must demonstrate the faith, or confidence, we have in ourselves. But even more important, any test of success should tell us something about the faith we have in God.

Faith is defined in the book of Hebrews as "the substance of things hoped for, the evidence of things not seen."[12] The act of faith becomes a reliance on or trust in something we don't fully possess. As we hope for something that's not seen, we show faith to the extent that we can live according to the reality of our unseen aspirations or hopes. Even if what we hope for doesn't quite work out the way we expect, we can show faith simply by acknowledging and accepting the hand of God in the final disposition of our hope.

I'm not sure it's possible to have true success without such faith. After all, as limited human beings we have little control over our own present, much less over our future. As James says in his New Testament epistle, "You do not know what will happen tomorrow. For what is your life? It is even a vapor that appears for a little time and then vanishes away."[13] And in the same vein, Proverbs says, "Many are the plans in the mind of a man, but it is the purpose of the LORD that will be established."[14]

Without the faith that there's some guiding hand or purpose behind our lives and careers, we become wide open to uncertainty, anxiety, and fear. We lose our sense of confidence and direction—and also our success. There can be no true success unless outward achievement is balanced by inner peace, satisfaction, and equanimity. On the other hand, when deep faith is present, a person can succeed and triumph in life even in the face of the severest challenges and pain.

One Baptist minister I know, named Arnie, was born with a bone disease that has weakened his entire skeleton. Throughout his life, his bones have regularly been fracturing and breaking, and he's spent much of his life under the care of a variety of doctors and nurses in hospitals. Among other things, his physicians do a lot of surgery to put pins into bones in an effort to strengthen them.

Arnie met his wife while he was attending seminary, and they were both assured that if they had children, the bone disease would not be passed on to them. But their first child has the same illness that Arnie suffers.

Despite his pain and disability and the disturbing knowledge that he passed the problem on to his child, Arnie has remained cheerful, buoyant, and productive. He carried on a very powerful and extensive pastoral ministry for a number of years in the Northeast. He also wrote a book about his feelings and experiences bringing up a daughter who suffers from the same disease that has racked his own body. And as if all this weren't enough, Arnie moved to the South and established a seminary to train ministers and church workers!

On one occasion I visited him at a hospital in New York when he was recovering from surgery. "This is my yearly operation, where I get some spikes driven into a part of my anatomy!" he said.

"How do you manage to keep so optimistic about life?" I asked, amazed at his ability to stay so happy and satisfied despite his discomfort and pain.

"I pray a lot," he responded. "Also, I keep very busy, and that keeps my mind off the physical discomfort. But you know, Tom, there's something more. I've come to believe that somewhere in the mystery of being 'created in God's image' there's a requirement that we must go through pain in this life. In a way, I feel closer to God, and I believe in some small way I have more of an understanding of His suffering because of what I've been through.

"Of course, when Jesus came into this world, He triumphed over an excruciating agony and death that I'll never have to face. But I find comfort in knowing that my suffering can't destroy me or my faith."

Arnie is one of the most successful people I've ever known for several reasons:

- He has lived in a way that is largely consistent with his basic principles and values.
- He has spent a great deal of time cultivating his important, in-depth personal relationships, including those with his family.
- He has accomplished many of his career goals.
- He has done it all with a solid faith—a faith that has given him ongoing joy and peace and has al-

lowed him to rise above physical pain and emotional anguish that would have devastated and immobilized almost anyone else.

Arnie can deal effectively with the present and look forward to the future with complete confidence for one major reason: He knows beyond any doubt that God is in charge of his work and his life.

So these are the five final tests that I apply to my life every so often just to see how I'm doing. Certainly, I may need to go into much greater depth in prayer, thought, and study when I find that somehow I haven't quite passed one of the tests. But as long as I can answer each of these questions with a yes, I know I'm generally on a course that reflects a relatively balanced and healthy attitude toward success.

CHAPTER ELEVEN

SUCCESSFUL . . . AND FREE!

When my son Nicholas was five years old, the time arrived for him to switch from the Jack and Jill School, a nursery school run by our parish in New York City, to another school. So my wife, Lys, and I began to struggle with some tough questions: Where should Nicholas go from here? What kind of education and environment would be best for him at this stage in his life?

As we went over our options, they seemed particularly difficult and, at times, even scary. For one thing, many of the most attractive places were frightfully expensive. Also, to get into the schools we were interested in, Nicholas had to take entrance exams, the sort of thing I thought had always been reserved for college students.

Finally, and perhaps most disturbing of all, we started hearing and reading things about how the right elementary school can put your child on "a fast track to the top! If you want your child to have a shot at the Ivy League, you'd better start making plans when he's five years old!"

Nicholas was, indeed, five. And even though I wasn't sure he'd want to go to Harvard or Yale, I didn't want to take a chance on having him accuse me of ruining his life when he was old enough for college.

To top it all off, a close friend, upon hearing of our impending decision, warned, "Do you want this little boy to be a success in life or not? The decision you make about his education now is going to determine whether he'll succeed!"

All of this, of course, created tremendous anxiety in parents who wanted the best for their youngster. I'd look into Nicholas's little face and think, *My goodness, do I want this boy to be a success or not? After all, I hold his future in my hands, don't I?*

When I stopped to think about it, I realized the truth. I didn't hold Nicholas's future in my hands. That was God's prerogative, not mine. *So it's happened to me once again,* I thought. The Success Cult—with its powerful potential for addiction to status, power, and money—had attacked me at my most vulnerable point, my concern about the future of my child.

I sat down in an easy chair and opened my Bible to that famous passage in the Sermon on the Mount, which I always find so comforting in moments like this: "But seek first the kingdom of God and His righteousness, and all these things shall be added to you."[1]

"That's what it's all about, isn't it, God?" I exclaimed. "You and Your kingdom first, and then, and then only, can there be a place for success—if success in the world's terms is part of Your plan at all."

We prayed and put the matter before God. In the end, we chose an academically excellent school in our neighborhood, which also had a supportive and nurturing environment. However, I knew the issue hadn't really been the choice of a school; it had been my attitude toward success. The conclusion I came to—that God was in charge of my son and his future—freed me from the need to try to control things I couldn't possibly control.

Of course, these ideas aren't original with me. The principle of putting God before worldly pursuits, such as careers and the drive to success, permeates Scripture. Furthermore, this principle guides many truly successful people and spiritual movements attuned to the demands of success in the present day.

THE FOCOLARE MOVEMENT

One movement in particular that has impressed me with its integration of faith and work is the Focolare Movement, a renewal force in the Roman Catholic church. The Focolare, which means "hearth" or "family fireside," began in 1943 in Italy in the midst of the terrible destruction wrought by World War II. A young woman, Chiara Lubich, realized that "God is the only One worth living for." As a result she began in a radical way to center her entire life on the gospel. Other young women soon followed her. Their ideal was to work toward the fulfillment of Jesus' last prayer to the Father, "That they all may be one."[2]

The Focolare Movement became an official part of the Catholic church by order of Pope John XXIII in 1962. But unlike the cloistered orders, the members open the doors of their movement to married people and families. Furthermore, they emphasize achieving unity and God's will in the midst of the pressures and trials of the working world.

Now, as we draw our consideration of success to a close, I'd like for us to consider some thoughts on achievement, work, and the will of God from Chiara Lubich. In a major address she delivered a few years ago in Italy to thousands of Focolarini, as those in the movement are called, she emphasized these basic principles of true success, which I've edited and sometimes paraphrased for our purposes.

Principle #1: We Are Called to Be Concerned First of All with the Kingdom of God.

Certainly, we must base the economic aspect of our lives on work, but we must not depend primarily on our work for the needs of our earthly existence. We must rely on God's providence. If we act as sons and daughters, God the Father will look after us.

Principle #2: We Should Have a High Concept of Work.

Why is this attitude important? Simply because God Himself considers work in this way. The Bible points out that it is characteristic of human beings to provide for sustenance and to work. Therefore, we *must* work.

The Word, when He became man, did not withdraw into solitude to meditate and pray in the thirty years of His private life. He was holy; He was God Himself; but He chose to be a worker. It is clear, then, that for God, work is an important aspect of our life; we should have to consider ourselves less human if we did not work. Since the Focolare Movement found its initial inspiration in the home of three workers—

Jesus, Mary, and Joseph—its members feel that in working they fulfill the will of God.

Principle #3: All Work Should Be Performed As Perfectly As Possible.

The members of the Focolare Movement are called to make every hour of work a masterpiece of precision, order, and harmony. They must love punctuality, be diligent, and make good use of their talents to improve their work. Just as for other reasons religious studies are obligatory for them, they must also continually perfect themselves in their jobs by studying material relevant to their professions.

In our day, for some parts of humanity, life has become nothing but a frenzy of work, a quest for super-perfection, which leaves no room for anything else in life. The movement does not make work the only thing necessary in life nor the only goal. What is supreme, what triumphs over all, is love.

Principle #4: We Should Work with a Certain Detachment from Our Professions.

Jesus said that a person who comes to Him must put aside mother, wife, children, brothers, sisters, and his own life, or he can't be a disciple.[3] So we must become to some degree detached from our jobs. We must be willing to put our jobs aside if they begin to take first place in our hearts.

Furthermore, a reward becomes available to those who make this kind of commitment or develop this sort of detachment. Jesus said that the person who has left his house, brother, sister, father, mother, children, or lands for His sake will be repaid a hundred times over and will also inherit eternal life.[4]

Principle #5: We Should Practice a Communion of Goods.

Some members of the Focolare achieve this communion in a total way. That is, they contribute their incomes and possessions to a common pool for the use of everyone in their community. Others achieve this material communion by making regular contributions from their surplus.

Principle #6: The Person Takes Precedence over Capital, Ownership, and Economic Structures.

Unfortunately, the center of our entire productive system has become production itself. The goods count, but not the person and his or her work. Often, the laborer's work has no meaning because it does not contribute toward the fulfillment of the person's potential as God's creature, for the development of creativity and intelligence. Work has taken on an alienating character.

It's necessary to reaffirm that the person takes precedence. It's necessary to create a work ethic that enables an individual, through work, to move closer to achieving fulfillment as a human being.

Principle #7: Human Beings Must Recognize Our Social Nature.

Unless human beings become aware of our social nature, we can't be completely human. According to Genesis there are at least three distinctive characteristics shared by humans: (1) our ability to have communion with God; (2) the requirement that we support ourselves through work; and (3) the interweaving of our relationships with other people.

Being social, in the truest sense, means loving

others as we love ourselves. Indeed, we must love them with a love inspired by Christ, a love that becomes reciprocal and generates unity. We must walk through life together, being of one heart and soul with others. Then our collective spirituality, which is ultimately derived from the gospel, can help us find solutions to the present problems of the working world.

Everyone, regardless of position, can participate in this spirituality—from the owners to the administrators, from the directors to the technicians, from the office workers to the outdoor laborers. Yet to build unity and solidarity with others, we must love our neighbors in such a way that they become one with us and with everyone else. In this common spirituality mutual love can lead to reciprocal understanding, to sharing the fatigue of others, to bearing the problems of others, and to seeking solutions together.

Principle #8: Finally, We Must Work toward Enhancing Our Spiritual Unity with Others.

It's impossibly idealistic to think that all by ourselves we can overcome all human weaknesses, ambitions, and impulses toward self-centeredness and achieve a perfect, harmonious unity with other workers. Human history is littered with the failed efforts of men and women who hoped to build the perfect world through their own efforts.

Who is capable of helping individual workers fully achieve greater social awareness of themselves as members of one great human family? Who can bring working people together after they have shattered their union with God through sin? Who can do it?

Only Christ can. Only with His love can we confidently build a world of lasting justice and peace. As far as work is concerned, it is only with His love that selfishness and hatred—often considered the law of society—can be eliminated. With His love, working communities will witness how unity, rather than conflict, can truly improve work. With His love, the life of society itself will be conceived not as a struggle against someone, but as a commitment to grow together.

A Christian vision of work and of history affirms that if we agree to place love for neighbor at the basis of our life and work, God will make us His partners in His work as Creator and Redeemer. On the seventh day God the Creator rested, almost as if to say that it was now *our* turn to continue His work! In loving, we live out the fact that we are made in the image of God, and therefore, our work becomes almost the work of God.

I've been deeply impressed by how members of the Focolare Movement strive to live and work by these and related principles. Sometimes, as I've spoken with them, I've sensed a kind of inner glow, even though I may know they've been through a particularly hard day on their jobs. Some are professionals, some managers, some secretaries, some laborers. They come from every walk of life, and like the rest of us, they constantly confront the meaning of careers, work, and success. Yet better than many people I know, they have discovered an integrating force for their lives that provides them with the possibility of achievement, but without the high risk of addiction to a distorted drive toward worldly success.

The Focolare Movement represents just one ap-

proach that can lead to a balanced, healthy view of
success. You may well find another way that enables
you to achieve the same end. In the final analysis, the
important thing to remember is that work—and that
ultimate fulfillment of work called career success—is
just one part of life.

TRUE SUCCESS

In the broadest sense, true success goes far beyond
career success. It encompasses satisfying achievements, rewards, and progress in *every* aspect of our
lives, including our relationship with God and our relationships with others.

To be sure, the typical working person will spend
more time on the job than on other activities or individuals, but quantity of time is no measure of importance and shouldn't serve as an ultimate standard as
you set personal priorities. Certainly, after you draft a
Rule of Life and highlight certain people or activities
as particularly worthy of your attention, you'll probably want to devote more time to them.

I'm reminded of one man who struggled for years to
establish a workable Rule of Life for himself. His
main problem was that he had found he was devoting
more attention than he liked to his work, and he was
neglecting his family and his spiritual development
and activities.

Finally, this man managed to put his life in balance
by establishing some definite guidelines for how he
would spend the hours of each week. For some people,
targeting a specific number of hours to spend on particular people or activities might seem too rigid or le-

galistic. But for him, experimenting with certain time commitments and then settling on the time allotments that "felt right" was just the approach he needed to get his life in balance.

Here are the hourly goals he finally chose:

- 55 hours—work
- 15 hours—children
- 15 hours—spouse
- 7 hours—private prayer and devotions
- 6 hours—service work, including helping individuals and church work
- 5 hours—worship, Bible study, and Christian fellowship

As you can see, the guidelines this man settled upon covered 103 hours out of the 168 hours available to him each week, and he also had to sleep and eat. Even with the adjustments he made through his Rule of Life, he still was spending most of his time at work, and this fact bothered him.

"I think I haven't gone quite far enough," he told me. "I think I should spend less time at work and more with God and my family."

"Wait a minute," I said. "How do you *feel*, now that you've made these adjustments?"

"I feel pretty good," he said.

"Are you meeting your obligations at work?"

"Yes."

"And how is your relationship with God getting along?"

"Wonderful! I'm discovering all sorts of things I never knew about prayer and spiritual growth."

"And what about your relationship with your wife and children?"

"Better than ever!"

"Then just relax and enjoy yourself!" I told him. "You've finally reached a real balance in your life. You're on the road to true success."

It's just one of the realities of our lives that we have to spend more time on the job than we do with any other individual or in any other activity. So don't worry if you find that, even after much thought and planning, you end up devoting most of your hours to work. That's to be expected.

There's no formula for achieving a proper balance, no sure-fire, guaranteed-to-work arrangement of the hours in your day or of your schedule. Each person's life is different, so your approach to true success is sure to be somewhat different from that of other people. The key consideration is what's going on inside you and what's happening in the important relationships in your life.

If you sense that your life is in balance and if you see your relationships with your loved ones, with your friends, and with God improving, you can be confident that you have managed to avoid the influence of the Success Cult. You're not addicted to the intoxicating, seductive aroma of distorted achievement. You're free!

NOTES

Chapter 1
1. Matthew 6:24.
2. Matthew 20:26.
3. Matthew 10:39.
4. Matthew 19:24.
5. 1 Timothy 6:9.
6. 1 Timothy 6:10.
7. Philippians 4:12.
8. Matthew 8:20.

Chapter 2
1. Genesis 3:17,19.
2. Proverbs 20.20, 14.23.
3. Proverbs 22:29.
4. See 1 Thessalonians 4:11–12.
5. 2 Thessalonians 3:10.
6. See Luke 6:38; 2 Corinthians 9:6.
7. See Romans 8:28–30.
8. 2 Timothy 1:9.

Chapter 3
1. The *New York Times Magazine*, August 16, 1987.
2. Ephesians 2:8–9.
3. Matthew 22:37.
4. See Leviticus 18:21; 20:2–5; 2 Kings 23:10.
5. The *New York Times*, October 15, 1987.
6. Luke 14:28.

Chapter 4
1. The *New York Times,* September 10, 1986.
2. The *Wall Street Journal,* September 16, 1986.
3. The *New York Times,* September 23, 1985.
4. The *New York Times,* July 28, 1985.

Chapter 5
1. The *New York Times Magazine,* October 26, 1986.
2. William Proctor, *The Templeton Touch* (Garden City, N.Y: Doubleday, 1983), pp. 5–9ff.
3. See Galatians 5:22.
4. *Newsweek,* July 22, 1985.
5. *The Great American Success Story* (Homewood, Ill.: Dow Jones-Irwin, 1986), p. 214. Henceforth, this book will be cited Gallup, *Story,* with the page number.
6. *Globe,* December 3, 1985.
7. The *Wall Street Journal,* May 20, 1987.
8. The *New York Times,* November 12, 1986.
9. The *New York Times,* June 15, 1986.
10. Gallup, *Story,* p. 211.
11. The *New York Times,* August 24, 1986.
12. The *Wall Street Journal,* November 12, 1986.
13. *New York Daily News,* May 8, 1987.
14. The *New York Times,* April 26, 1987.
15. Dustin Beall Smith, "A Promise of Renewal," The *New York Times Magazine,* July 28, 1987.

Chapter 6
1. The *New York Times Magazine,* September 29, 1985.
2. The *New York Times,* October 6, 1985.
3. D. Mackenzie Brown, *Ultimate Concern: Tillich in Dialogue*
4. The *New York Times Magazine,* January 4, 1987.
5. The *Wall Street Journal,* May 1, 1986.
6. John 10:10.

Chapter 7
1. Gallup, *Story,* p. 233.
2. *Parade* magazine, July 7, 1985.
3. Mark 10:43.

4. John 13:3–11.
5. Donald V. Seibert, *The Ethical Executive* (New York: Cornerstone Library, Simon & Schuster, 1984), p. 206.
6. Seibert, *The Ethical Executive*, p. 207.

Chapter 8
1. *Business Week*, August 31, 1987.
2. Reported in The *Wall Street Journal*, October 15, 1985.
3. *New York Daily News*, August 19, 1986.
4. *Business Week*, June 2, 1986.
5. *Parade* magazine, March 8, 1987.
6. *Parade* magazine, July 26, 1987.
7. The *New York Times*, September 28, 1987.
8. The *New York Times Magazine*, September 27, 1987.

Chapter 9
1. The *New York Times*, April 17, 1987.
2. *New York Daily News*, April 5, 1987.
3. The *New York Times*, May 21, 1987.
4. The *New York Times*, May 12, 1987.
5. From *Passing Shots* (New York: McGraw-Hill, 1986).
6. The *New York Times*, July 4, 1985.

Chapter 10
1. Proverbs 12:27 RSV.
2. Proverbs 14:23 RSV.
3. The *Wall Street Journal*, December 16, 1986.
4. Gallup, *Story*, p. 220.
5. The *New York Times Magazine*, September 28, 1986.
6. *New York Daily News*, February 15, 1987.
7. The *Wall Street Journal*, September 23, 1985.
8. "Sacrificing Part of Your Vacation May Win No Credit With the Boss," The *Wall Street Journal*, December 29, 1986.
9. *Parade* magazine, March 29, 1987.
10. Matthew 6:34.
11. See Acts 2:42.
12. Hebrews 11:1.
13. James 4:14.
14. Proverbs 19:21 RSV.

Chapter 11
1. Matthew 6:33.
2. John 17:21.
3. See Luke 14:26.
4. See Matthew 19:29.